Centerville Library
Washington-Centerville Public Library
Centerville, Ohio

DISCARD

W9-BVV-480

a SAVOR THE SOUTH® *cookbook*

Ham

a SAVOR THE SOUTH® *cookbook*

Ham

DAMON LEE FOWLER

The University of North Carolina Press CHAPEL HILL

© 2017 The University of North Carolina Press
All rights reserved. Manufactured in the United States of America.
SAVOR THE SOUTH® is a registered trademark of the
University of North Carolina Press, Inc.
Designed by Kimberly Bryant and set in Miller and
Calluna Sans types by Rebecca Evans.

The University of North Carolina Press has been
a member of the Green Press Initiative since 2003.

Cover illustration © istockphoto.com/zhekos

Library of Congress Cataloging-in-Publication Data
Names: Fowler, Damon Lee, author.
Title: Ham / Damon Lee Fowler.
Other titles: Savor the South cookbook.
Description: Chapel Hill : The University of North Carolina
Press, [2017] | Series: A savor the South cookbook
Identifiers: LCCN 2017015401| ISBN 9781469635897
(cloth : alk. paper) | ISBN 9781469635903 (ebook)
Subjects: LCSH: Cooking (Ham) | Cooking, American—
Southern style. | LCGFT: Cookbooks.
Classification: LCC TX749.5.H35 F69 2017 | DDC 641.3/64—dc23
LC record available at https://lccn.loc.gov/2017015401

*For Sam and Donna Edwards and the
folks at Edwards Virginia Smokehouse in Surry,
Virginia, in honor of their commitment to
fine southern-cured hams*

And, as always, for Timothy

Contents

Introduction

he wag who first defined eternity as "two people and a ham" is lost to time: Though often credited to mid-twentieth-century wit Dorothy Parker, there's actually no record of when or if she ever said it. But there's one thing you can bet on: whoever did say it wasn't a southerner.

While the hindquarters of swine have been preserved in salt the world over for thousands of years, there is probably no other place on earth, except possibly Italy and Spain, where ham is as celebrated or integral to the cuisine as it is in the American South.

To begin to understand the place that this iconic food holds in the hearts of the South and its food history, one has only to step into the two-hundred-year-old smokehouse in the South dependency of Thomas Jefferson's beloved Monticello and take a deep breath. More than a century after the last hams were hung to smoke in that chamber, the aroma of salt, smoke, and air-dried pork still permeates the rough masonry walls and red clay floor, filling the air with its earthy perfume. Likewise, even after four centuries and the inevitable transformations that immigration and globalization have brought to the South's many cultures and cuisines, that same earthy perfume lingers in kitchens throughout the region.

Although swine aren't native to North America, they've been an integral part of the South and its cookery from the earliest days of European colonization. Pigs are believed to have been introduced to the region in Florida and coastal Georgia by Spanish colonials in the late sixteenth century. But even before the animals themselves set foot on American soil, their dry-salted and/or pickled (brine-cured) flesh was surely part of the provisions those settlers brought with them, as it would have been a few years later for the first permanent English settlers at Jamestown, Virginia. In those shaky early days, the colonists depended largely on imported provisions, but soon they were raising, slaughtering, and preserving their own pigs.

The advantage of swine for these colonial outposts was that they didn't need a lot of attention to thrive. Pigs will eat just about anything and everything, and can pretty much be left to fend for themselves. Often they were simply turned loose (or got loose) to forage in the forests, and a lot of them stayed there. The wild boars that now populate the South's woodlands (and which, thanks in part to the urbanization of their habitats, have today become such a menace) are all descended from those early domestic animals that just never came back home.

The one disadvantage of pork, particularly in those days before cold storage, is that it's far more perishable than any other meat and back then had to be eaten pretty much as soon as it was slaughtered. This was why hog-killing time occurred in autumn with the first cold snap. But that little defect disappeared as soon as the meat was exposed to salt. Once it's properly cured and stored, it'll keep for months, even years, without refrigeration. In a largely rural economy, where most families were farmers raising their own food and cold storage consisted of a spring house and root cellar, having fresh meat every single day would've meant slaughtering an animal almost every day, something that would have been impractical even if it was possible. Cured pork therefore became a critical source of animal protein and a staple in every diet, whether the household was rich or poor, at liberty or enslaved.

Edmund Bacon, Thomas Jefferson's estate overseer from 1806 to 1822, wrote that his master often told him that the weekly ration of salt pork for each of his enslaved workers was more than he could have consumed in six months. That remark is usually quoted as evidence of Jefferson's simple and largely vegetarian diet, but in the bigger picture it also tells us that salt pork was the fuel that kept Monticello, and indeed, every other plantation and farm in the South, going.

And while Jefferson may not have partaken of it very often, one of the well-aged hams from that aromatic smokehouse, boiled and toasted (that is, carefully poached in water to cover and then coated with crumbs and browned in the oven) would have been a fixture on Monticello's table. Martha Washington, whose social and political position required her to entertain a steady stream of visitors at Mount Vernon, was reputed to have ordered a ham from the kitchen almost every single day. And scarcely half a century later, Annabella Hill, author of *Mrs. Hill's New Cook Book* (1867) and one of the nineteenth century's great chroniclers of southern cookery, referred to boiled ham as "our favorite every-day dish."

The proper curing and storing of pork, particularly of hams, was therefore a critical skill. Not surprisingly, the most ubiquitous, lengthy, and detailed recipes, both in published southern cookbooks beginning with Mary Randolph's *The Virginia Housewife* (1824) and in the manuscript household notebooks from the first three centuries of our history, are for curing a ham. The only recipes that were longer were the ones that detailed the proper way to clean, boil, and toast the thing.

To be sure, there's an art to the salt-curing process, especially of hams, but fortunately, mastering the necessary techniques and skills is a pretty straightforward business. Even so, when the very survival of the family was at stake, it was not a job that could be left to careless hands.

As late as my own childhood in the mid-twentieth century, the art of ham-curing was still a point of pride, and continued to thrive in rural areas. Each community often boasted its own champion. But as urbanization has crept across the southern landscape over the last half century, that art has dwindled faster than the acreage of land that is still under cultivation. By the time my first cookbook was published near the end of the twentieth century, there were few families whose livelihood depended entirely (or even mostly) on a farm, and of those, fewer still that could boast a member who could even tell you how a ham was cured in theory, let alone do it.

Happily, the last two decades have seen what I very much hope is a reversal of that trend. Today there's a resurgence of interest in the art of curing, and very fine hams and other salt-cured pork products are now being put forth by artisanal producers from Virginia, the Carolinas, Georgia, Kentucky, and Tennessee. The numbers are still small, but that they're continuing to grow is hopeful.

Part and parcel of that renewed interest in the art of curing is concern for the animals from which the hams that we cure have come. The old saying that we are what we eat may seem a bit hackneyed, but it sounds that way because it's true. And what's true for us is equally true for a pig. A part of the character of some of the world's most famed hams has historically been attributed to what the pigs were fed, from the cheese whey that was purported to have given prosciutto di Parma its luscious creaminess to the acorns, peanuts, and pecans that have variously been credited with the intense flavor of hams in the South. Whether those things really had all that much to do with the unique character of each of these hams, a good deal of the quality and flavor of the meat actually will depend on how the animal from which it came was treated and fed before it was led away to be slaughtered.

I will never forget the moment all that was brought home to me. It was a cool, sunny autumn afternoon at a conference on the art of pasture-raising animals and we were getting ready to judge a friendly barbecue competition. As we made the rounds of the farmer/pit-masters, one of them handed me a forkful of slow-smoked barbecued pork. The meat was from an heirloom-breed Berkshire pig that had been allowed to supplement its natural diet by foraging at will. I took a bite, closed my eyes, and was enveloped in a sudden rush of memory so sharp and happy that I literally burst into tears before I could get control of myself.

In my childhood, that was how all the pork that we ate tasted. My dad is a minister and we didn't farm, but most of our neighbors did: The fresh meat, sausages, bacon, and hams that they shared with us were all from old breeds of pigs that had enjoyed a natural diet of the food that grew all around them and had been allowed to wallow happily in all the mud they could possibly want. I took the flavor of the meat from those pigs for granted. But after I left home, without my realizing it, my palate gradually became accustomed to the bland taste of pork from the newer breeds of mass-farmed pigs that had been fed on nothing but bland commercial feed and raised in crowded pens where they were lucky to lie down, let alone wallow. I had never thought about it until the intense flavor of that one bite of barbecue met with my tongue, a sharply poignant, even heartbreaking reminder of what we had lost.

And that's without delving into the negative impact that the mass farming of animals like pigs, chickens, and cattle has on our environment.

Now, I'm not suggesting that you turn your backyard into a pigsty, take up hauling a slop bucket, and convert your garage into a smokehouse. But if you do take the time and go to the extra expense of seeking out and procuring hams and other pork products from naturally raised animals, I can promise that your efforts will be more than amply rewarded.

But back to that southern ham: those words inevitably conjure images of the legendary dry-cured and aged joints that most southerners call country ham, such as those that came from Monticello's smokehouse, but a glance at contemporary southern cookbooks, restaurant menus, and modern markets tell a different story. Our affection for ham is no longer confined to such narrow historical or regional boundaries—if, indeed, it ever was.

We love ham just about any and every way it's made and cooked: brine- or dry-cured, smoked or not, boiled, baked, glazed, not glazed, honey-baked and spiral-cut, thinly sliced and piled into biscuits or on sourdough bread, fried and served up with grits and red-eye gravy, deviled, creamed, as added savor for dozens of soups, casseroles, meat, poultry, and seafood dishes, and, yes, as that notoriously universal seasoning in the vegetable pot.

We also love ham in gumbo, mixed with rice in jambalayas and pilaus, and tossed into a salad as an accent or even as the main ingredient, variously seasoned, depending on the part of the South that you find yourself, with sweet pickles, olives, dill pickles, capers, sweet peppers, and even almonds, peanuts, and pecans. We love it cut into thick center-cut steaks, mellowed by baking them in our own Coca-Cola or brightened by pan-broiling them with fresh Florida orange juice.

Those are just a few of the hundreds of ways that southern cooks have traditionally loved to prepare ham, and you'll find as many of them between the covers of this book as I could fit.

But as the South continues to evolve and its population takes on an ethnic diversity that's truly global, southern cooks have gone beyond those traditional ways of savoring ham to embrace an international repertory of dishes. We now love the buttery richness of dry-cured ham when sliced wafer-thin to enwrap fresh figs or melon or to blanket sage-scented scaloppine, its nutty intensity when diced to stud fried rice or fragrant lo mein, its suave elegance when tucked into classic cordon bleu, and its earthy satisfaction piled into a crusty croque monsieur or Cuban sandwich. You'll therefore find on these pages many international dishes that have found a home in the hearts and kitchens of today's southern cooks.

But before we explore and savor all these lovely things, let's be clear about what we mean when we say ham.

Ham Basics

Little more than thirty years ago, no one would have thought it necessary to begin a book about ham with a definition of its subject. But as the word has been carelessly appropriated to name all manner of pink, salty, artificially smoky foodstuffs made from poultry, soybeans, and goodness knows what else, "ham" is in grave danger of losing its original meaning. To make sure that we're all on the same page, then, here's a short glossary of terms that readers may find useful.

HAM Throughout this book, the word is used to describe only the salt-cured hindquarter of a pig or a cut of the meat from said hindquarter. Historically, the word was first used to name the hind parts of all four-legged animals. It derives from the Old English and Old High German words for the hollow behind the knee or the buttocks and thigh portion of the leg, the latter especially as a cut of meat. In the culinary world, the word eventually came to be used almost exclusively to mean the hindquarter of a pig, and eventually to mean one that had been preserved with salt.

There are two primary ways of so curing hams: dry-curing and brine-curing.

Dry-curing is a process in which the ham is rubbed with dry salt and left to lie until much of its moisture has been drawn out. Sometimes the hams are stacked or otherwise weighted to speed up the process. They're then hung in a well-ventilated but protected shelter to air dry, over the process losing even more of their natural moisture. The salt-curing mixture may be supplemented with sugar and spices, and the hams may be finished by cold-smoking them with smoldering hardwood. The ham may also be finished by rubbing it with spices or hardwood ashes. Today there are at least thirty-six kinds of dry-cured hams, distributed over at least fifteen countries, whose names and ties to a place of origin are protected by law. The best known of these include the South's own Smithfield hams, Italy's prosciutto (notably prosciutto di Parma), Spain's Serrano ham (jamón serrano), Iberian ham (Spain's jamón ibérico and Portugal's presunto ibérico), Germany's Westfälischer Schinken (Westphalian ham), and China's huotui.

Brine-curing is a process in which the ham is cured by submerging it in a heavy brine, a method that used to be known as pickling. Though in the South this method was traditionally used for other cuts of pork, today, in the broader United States, brine-cured hams are the most common. Usually (but not always) they're finished with smoke or injected with smoke flavoring. When the label of a brine-cured ham reads "water added" it means that it has been injected with a brine solution that can make up as much as 10 percent of its weight. Most of the supermarket and deli sandwich hams in the United States today are brine-cured hams with water added. Another well-known example of brine-cured ham is Brazil's presunto.

COUNTRY HAM This is just another name for a dry-cured ham from the South that has almost always been finished by cold-smoking and is often rubbed with hardwood ashes and/or black pepper as a preservative. It's not to be confused with Peruvian country ham (jamón del pais peruano), which is lightly brined and cooked with spices that actually turn it yellow.

FRESH HAM This refers not to an uncooked cured ham but to a freshly butchered leg of pork.

OLD HAM This is a term used mostly in the South for a dry-cured ham that has been aged for at least eighteen months or up to two years. In some parts of the South, the most revered of these is aged for a full three years. Most old hams were traditionally smoked, but as artisanal cure-masters across our region have begun to adapt Italian, Spanish, and Portuguese styles into their curing methods, creating prosciutto-, Serrano-, and Iberian-style hams with a southern drawl, there are increasing numbers of fine southern old hams that never see the inside of a smokehouse, and many of them rival their European counterparts.

PICNIC HAM Technically this isn't a ham but the shoulder and foreleg cut of the pig. It can be fresh, dry-cured, or brine-cured.

HAM HOCK A cut from the lower shank joint of the ham, roughly corresponding to our ankle. In the United States, ham hocks are usually smoked. They're used for stock and as a flavoring for soup, beans, and hearty greens such as cabbage, collards, kale, and turnip tops.

HAM KNUCKLE Though in butcher's terms knuckle can also refer to any cut of meat near the joint, with ham it always means the joint itself. Usually smoked and used in the same way as hocks, knuckles are often sold sawn into thick slices.

HAM STEAK Traditionally referring to a thick, bone-in center-cut slab that is cut perpendicular to the bone, today this means any slice of ham that's at least half an inch thick.

SEASONING PIECES In the South, these scrap chunks of dry-cured ham are sold as a seasoning for soups and stocks, beans, and hearty vegetables.

CENTER-CUT SLICES Thin slices of dry-cured ham cut perpendicular to the bone from the meaty center, these may be sold with or without the round bone at the center.

BOILED HAM In the market, this means any ham that's fully cooked in water (although hams so labeled are usually brine-cured). At home, it means a ham poached in liquid (see page 14).

CANNED HAM Boned, trimmed, and sometimes compressed ham that has been cooked and canned in one large piece.

PRESSED HAM A cooked, compressed block made from small trimmed pieces or shreds of ham, usually sold presliced.

A NOTE ON NITRATES AND NITRITES

Nitrates and nitrites are added to cured meat both to set its color and to act as a preservative and antimicrobial. Though only very small amounts of these natural compounds are used in curing meat, there has recently been some concern about their place in a healthy diet. Though specific medical problems may warrant avoiding them altogether, like most things in life, moderation appears to be the key to consuming foods that contain them.

Sodium nitrate, a naturally occurring compound of sodium, nitrogen, and oxygen, is the most commonly used of these compounds. Trace amounts of it are a natural component of many plant foods. It's the curing component that sets the ham's rosy-pink or deep, ruddy-red color.

Potassium nitrate, commonly known as "saltpeter," is a compound of potassium and nitrogen that has a wide range of uses, from food preservative to fertilizer to gunpowder and other explosives. Its job in curing was to set and preserve color and to prevent botulism. But while still used in some charcuterie and in brined meats like corned beef, its use in ham has waned in modern times because it doesn't produce the consistent results that sodium nitrates and nitrites do.

Sodium nitrite is an inorganic compound of sodium and nitrite that's essential to the world of pharmaceuticals. It's used in food preservation as an antimicrobial to prevent botulism and rancidity. While very small amounts are useful in medicine and food preservation, large doses of this compound can be toxic (it's also used in pesticides). If you choose to avoid cured meat that contains nitrites, be aware that nitrite-free products have a limited shelf life. You should use extra care in storing and using nitrite-free products within their manufacturer's recommendations.

Techniques and Basic Recipes

Sautéing, frying, pan-frying, and pan-broiling: These techniques are often confused with one another, but while all four may involve a shallow pan or skillet, there the resemblance ends.

SAUTÉING

The word "sauté" is from the French verb *sauter*, meaning "to jump," and in culinary terms, a proper sauté is when food is quite literally "jumping" in the pan so that it cooks evenly—that is, the cook is constantly agitating it either by shaking the pan, by stirring with a spatula or spoon, or by regularly flipping it with a spatula or pair of tongs. It's often mistranslated as "to lightly fry," but that's not really an accurate description of what happens. This technique is used for smaller pieces of ham—for browning diced or julienned ham or for regularly turning thin medallions of country ham as they cook.

FRYING AND PAN-FRYING

To fry is to cook in boiling fat, either by submerging the food in it or by covering it halfway in a shallow frying pan. The latter is often called pan-frying. In ham cookery, this technique is used for both thick and thin slices and croquettes and for foods stuffed with ham.

PAN-BROILING

Before gas and electric ranges introduced a heat source that could be over rather than under the food, broiling was done on a grate over hot coals, the same technique that we call grilling today. Pan-broiling imitates that older technique. The food is cooked in a heavy-bottomed skillet to which very little or no fat has been added. The food is usually turned only once or at most twice. Pan-broiling is primarily used for thick ham steaks (see page 106).

BAKING

This is cooking in an enclosed chamber so that the food is surrounded by moist heat, either in a covered casserole on the stovetop or in a covered or open pan in the oven, with enough liquid added to keep the air moist with steam. The technique mainly is used for cooking a whole ham or a large ham butt or shank portion. Dry-cured hams are often first poached in simmering water before they're baked, but they're also sometimes baked in a covered pan.

BOILING

The use of this term in ham cookery harkens back to the days when "boiling" meant anything from a rolling clip to a gentle simmer, so it's misleading. As is true with any meat, a properly boiled ham is never allowed to actually boil. The water is brought slowly to a bare simmer, and, just as the bubbles begin to break the surface, the heat is adjusted so that the water merely shimmers, with only an occasional bubble breaking its surface. This technique is mostly used for cooking a whole dry-cured ham.

GLAZING AND TOASTING

These common finishes for whole hams have more to do with presentation than flavor. The cooked ham is skinned, some of its fat is removed, and its surface is coated and run back into a hot oven. The coating for glazing is usually a mixture of sugar and spices and sometimes wine, whiskey, or fruit juice. Sometimes bread crumbs or finely chopped nuts are added for body. The coating for toasting is dry bread crumbs or cracker crumbs, sometimes with spices and/or finely chopped nuts mixed in. The ham is brushed with an egg wash and then generously coated with the crumb mixture.

To Bake a Ham

Baking a whole ham in a covered pan, with just enough liquid to keep it moist, is the ideal way to prepare a whole brine-cured smoked ham. But many aficionados of country hams, particularly the celebrated Smithfield and artisan-cured hams from Virginia, Kentucky, Tennessee, North Carolina, and Georgia, prefer this method for those as well. The results are saltier than a boiled ham, so if you think the extra salt will be a bit too intense for your taste, before cooking it, soak the ham overnight as directed on page 15).

SERVES 20

One dry-cured ("country") ham (11–14 pounds),
  a whole portion of a regular smoked ham (12–18 pounds),
  or butt portion of a regular smoked ham (11–13 pounds)
2 cups water
1 cup bourbon or 1 (12-ounce) bottle Coca-Cola (optional)

Position a rack in the center of the oven and preheat to 325°.

If using a dry-cured ham, prepare it as directed on page 14.

Fit a rack into a large covered roaster or baking pan, add the water and the bourbon or Coca-Cola, if using, and put the ham skin-side up on the rack. Bake for 2½–3 hours or to an internal temperature of 145–160°.

Remove the ham from the oven and let it cool enough to handle. Remove the rind and some of the fat with a sharp knife, but leave a good layer of fat on all sides. You can serve it as it is, or you can toast or glaze it. If not serving it right away, cover and refrigerate it. To toast or glaze it, see page 16 or 17.

To Boil (Poach) a Dry-Cured Southern Country Ham

Boiling a whole country ham well is an art that has almost been lost to the modern world, since few of us have the kind of large household or social calendar that warrants keeping a whole ham on hand. But when you need to pull out the stops for a party, a whole country ham is the way to do it. Remember that the ham should never actually boil but should poach gently in liquid that is kept at a bare simmer. That liquid can simply be water, but for truly special occasions southern cooks often spike the water with sparkling wine, whiskey, or even Coca-Cola. Serve it sliced wafer-thin, with prepared English or French Dijon-style mustard, horseradish sauce, and/or chutney.

Traditionally, old hams were soaked overnight in cold water to take out some of the salt and partly rehydrate the meat—the same idea as presoaking dried legumes. But many old ham lovers frown on this process, arguing that the intense, concentrated flavor and saltiness are part of the point of a good ham. But if you prefer it to be milder, by all means soak it.

SERVES ABOUT 25–30

---

1 whole dry-cured (country) ham, weighing about
   11–14 pounds
1 bottle dry champagne, 2 cups bourbon,
   or 2 (12-ounce) bottles Coca-Cola (optional)

Under cold running water, scrub the ham all over with a stiff brush to remove all mold. If you're soaking the ham, put it in a large tub and cover it completely with cold water. Soak it for at least 8 hours, or for as long as 24–48 hours if the ham is especially old, changing the water 2 to 3 times during the process. Drain and wipe it down.

Put the ham in a large, deep oval pot that will hold it and enough water to cover it. If you're using one of the flavoring liquids, pour it over the ham, then add enough cold water to completely cover it by at least an inch. Turn on the heat to medium low and let it come slowly to the boiling point, skimming off any scum that rises, 45 minutes to an hour.

Reduce the heat to a barely perceptible simmer. The steam bubbles should only occasionally and barely break the surface of the water. Never allow it to actually boil. Simmer gently until just tender, 3–4 hours. Turn off the heat and let the ham cool in the cooking water.

Lift the ham from its cooking liquid. Remove the rind and some of the fat with a sharp knife, but leave a good layer of fat on all sides. You can serve it as it is, or you can toast or glaze it. If not serving it right away, cover and refrigerate it. To toast or glaze it, see To Toast a Fully Cooked Ham (page 16) or To Glaze a Fully Cooked Ham (page 17).

To Toast a Fully Cooked Ham

SERVES 12–25

---

1 whole dry-cured country ham, cooked as directed on
  page 13 or 14
1 large egg, well beaten
About 1 cup fine, dry bread crumbs or cracker crumbs

Position a rack in the center of the oven and preheat to 400°.
If the ham has been refrigerated, let it sit for at least 30 minutes at room temperature before toasting it. Put the ham in a
rimmed baking or roasting pan, skin-side up, and brush its fat
with the egg. Dust all sides well with the crumbs, pressing to
help them stick.

Bake, uncovered, until lightly browned, about 30–45 minutes.
Let it rest for half an hour before carving and cut it with a razor-
sharp knife into the thinnest possible slices.

To Glaze a Fully Cooked Ham

Many whole brine-cured hams are sold fully cooked, often pre-sliced with a spiral slicer for foolproof carving. These hams can be served at room temperature or cold, or they can be reheated and glazed. This is really two recipes in one: you can omit the liquid called for and make a dry sugar compound that's rubbed over the ham's surface, or add liquid for a glaze that's brushed on.

SERVES 12–25

---

1 fully-cooked whole ham (about 12–18 pounds) or
    butt portion (11–13 pounds)
½ cup medium-dry sherry or apple or pineapple juice
    (optional)
½ cup bourbon (optional)
1½ cups light brown sugar
3 teaspoons dry mustard
Ground cayenne pepper

Position a rack in the center of the oven and preheat to 400°. If the ham has been refrigerated, let it sit for at least 30 minutes at room temperature before continuing. Put the ham in a rimmed baking or roasting pan, skin-side up, and if you like score the fat in a crisscross pattern.

If you're not including the optional liquids (sherry or fruit juice and bourbon), skip to the next step. If including them, combine them in a saucepan and bring them to a boil over medium heat. Cook until it is reduced by half. Turn off the heat.

Mix together the brown sugar, mustard, and a large pinch of cayenne in a bowl. If using the reduced liquid mixture, mix it with the sugar mixture to make a paste.

Rub the sugar mixture all over the ham and bake until its glazed and browned, about 30–45 minutes. Let it rest in the pan at least 20 minutes, then carefully transfer it to a platter to carve and serve.

Sautéed Southern Country Ham with Redeye Gravy

There are two schools of thought on the best way to successfully cook slices of country ham: one is lightly and quickly, the other is the opposite extreme—gently and slowly. In my book Classical Southern Cooking, *I gave the light and quick method, to which my grandmother, of the low-and-slow school, took a dim view, so here's her way of doing it. This is called sautéed because the ham is kept moving; that is, it's frequently turned so that it cooks evenly. But it differs from true sautéing since the heat for that technique is generally lively, while here it's low and gentle.*

In the old days, this dish was just as likely to turn up on the supper table as at breakfast time, especially on chilly autumn and winter nights. Sometimes fried eggs will accompany it (see page 51), but grits are always offered, and they should be simmered until thick enough to handle the gravy.

SERVES 4

---

1 pound uncooked country ham, sliced thin (see Note)
Bacon drippings or vegetable oil, as needed
About ½ cup plain, all-purpose flour
¼ cup strong tea or coffee
¾ cup boiling water
Whole black pepper in a mill

If the ham is especially old and rich, soak it in water to cover for about 10 minutes. Drain and pat it dry. Trim the fat from it and cut each slice into medallions about 2 inches across. Spread the flour on a plate and put it by the stove.

Rub a cast-iron or heavy-bottomed skillet with a piece of the fat trimmings, add all the trimmings to the pan, and turn on the heat to medium. When the fat is rendered, remove the cracklings and reduce the heat to medium low. If there isn't enough fat to film the bottom of the pan, add bacon drippings or oil as needed. Alternatively, you may omit rendering the fat altogether and simply film the bottom of the pan with bacon drippings or vegetable oil.

Turn the ham slices lightly in the flour, shake off the excess, and add them to the pan. Sauté, turning frequently, until the outer surface is lightly browned and the ham is tender, 8–10 minutes. Transfer the ham to a warm platter.

Deglaze the pan with the tea or coffee and bring it to a boil. Add the water, stirring and scraping to loosen any cooking residue, and continue cooking until the gravy is lightly reduced and thickened. Season to taste with pepper and pour the gravy into a sauceboat. Serve at once, passing the ham and gravy separately.

NOTE ✳ You can also use slices of boiled or baked ham. Trim off most of the fat. Put enough of the fat in a skillet to make about a tablespoon of fat per serving of ham. Render it over medium-low heat, remove the cracklings, and add the sliced ham. Cook slowly for about 5 minutes, turning frequently, until the slices are heated through and lightly colored. Spoon off any excess fat and make the redeye gravy as directed above.

Ham Crisps

On a sunny but cool autumn afternoon, a group of American journalists crowded into the small but picturesque kitchen of a little villa in the hill country near Parma, where a classically trained Parmigiani chef gave us an intense lesson in cooking with his native city's two most famous food products: prosciutto and Parmigiano-Reggiano cheese. We learned about and tasted some amazing stuff, but the thing we couldn't stop talking about (or eating) was a crisp little wafer of prosciutto made simply by dropping tissue-thin sheets of the stuff onto a hot, lightly oiled pan.

Use this as you would cooked bacon, especially in a BLT or an avocado sandwich, or use it as a garnish/accompaniment for chilled melon or avocado soup.

SERVES 3–4

Canola or other vegetable oil or olive oil (not extra-virgin)
4 ounces very thinly sliced prosciutto di Parma, jamón
serrano, jamón ibérico, or dry-aged country ham

Brush a heavy, nonstick skillet or well-seasoned iron skillet with oil and warm it over medium heat. When it's moderately hot, lay in a couple of slices of the ham. They should lightly sizzle and immediately start to bubble. Cook until they're lightly colored on the bottom, then turn and continue cooking until lightly colored on both sides and crisp, about 2 minutes per side.

Remove the crisped ham from the pan and let it cool on paper towels while you repeat with the remaining ham. If making it more than an hour ahead, let it completely cool before storing it in an airtight plastic or tin container, but use it the day you make it.

Appetizers and Soups

Southerners have long known that nothing can tease and pique the appetite quite like a savory bite of ham. Long before there was any such thing as "cocktail hour," beaten biscuits or buttermilk biscuits stuffed with thinly sliced baked ham, or biscuits or toast points and a crock of deviled ham, might be offered as a gesture of hospitality for drop-in company between meals or for invited company before one. As the cocktail hour became popular both as a prelude to dinner and as a form of entertainment in itself, ham came out from between those biscuits to appear in countless new cocktail canapes.

We're not, of course, alone in the knowledge of ham's gift for stirring appetites. It's also an indispensable part of Spanish tapas, Swedish smorgasbords, and Italian antipasti. In today's South, many of the dishes from those traditions have joined the time-honored ham biscuit and other regional staples like pickled okra and pimiento cheese to become fixtures on many southern appetizer trays.

When it comes to the soup kettle, as far as many southern cooks are concerned, ham is to soup what gin is to martinis: You can make one without it, but in our estimation it's going to be a thin shadow of what it might have been. Ham broth is the base for most classic southern vegetable soups, seafood soups, and gumbos and is used as a seasoning base for beans and hearty greens like cabbage, collards, and kale and for making savory dumplings. And as immigrants from other cultures settle into the South and make it home, ham-based soups with Asian, Spanish, Italian, and Latin American accents have further enriched our repertory.

Hardwood-Grilled
Prosciutto-Wrapped Shrimp

Bacon-wrapped shrimp has lately become a popular cocktail hors d'oeuvres and is a lovely idea, but it does have one drawback: by the time the bacon is crisp, even when it has been blanched first, the shrimp is often overcooked and tough. Paper-thin slices of ham, on the other hand, cook in a flash and, when grilled over hardwood, lend almost the same flavor as bacon without that drawback.

SERVES 4 AS A MAIN DISH OR 6–8 AS AN APPETIZER

1¼ pounds jumbo or extra-large shrimp
2 ounces thinly sliced prosciutto
2 large garlic cloves, lightly crushed and peeled
¼ cup olive, peanut, or canola oil
2 lemons cut into wedges

Soak 8- to 10-inch bamboo skewers in water to cover for 30 minutes. Peel and devein the shrimp. Cut each piece of prosciutto in half lengthwise. Wrap 1 piece of prosciutto around each shrimp and thread them onto skewers, about 2–3 per skewer. Heat the garlic and oil in a small pan over medium-low heat until the garlic is golden. Turn off the heat, let it sit for about 5 minutes, then remove and discard the garlic.

Prepare the grill with hardwood coals (not briquettes) and ignite them; let the coals burn to a medium-hot fire. Position the grill grid about 6–8 inches above the heat. Brush the shrimp with the garlic oil and grill, turning once, until the shrimp are just cooked through and the prosciutto is lightly crisped, 3–4 minutes. Serve immediately with lemon wedges.

Vidalia Sweet Onions
Stuffed with Ham and Herbs

Sweet onions and ham are another natural and popular pairing in southern kitchens. Here, the onions are hollowed out to form a sweet casing for a robust filling of ham and herbs. Though more commonly served as a sit-down first course for a more formal meal, these are substantial enough to serve as a main dish for lunch or supper yet light enough to serve as a side dish with a simple roast chicken or grilled steak.

SERVES 4

4 large Vidalia or other sweet yellow onions such as Bermuda
1 cup minced cooked ham, preferably country ham
½ cup soft bread crumbs
1 tablespoon minced fresh sage
1 tablespoon minced fresh thyme
1 tablespoon unsalted butter, melted, plus 3–6 tablespoons
    cold unsalted butter, cut into bits
Whole nutmeg in a grater
Whole black pepper in a mill
About 2 cups chicken broth
1 tablespoon chopped flat-leaf (Italian) parsley

Peel the outer skins from the onions, but don't cut off the root or stem. Bring a large stockpot of water to a boil, add the onions, and bring back to a boil. Reduce the heat and simmer until the onions are nearly tender. Depending on the size, this could take anywhere from 20 to 45 minutes.

Position a rack in the center of the oven and preheat to 350°. While the onions simmer, mix together the ham, bread crumbs, sage, thyme, and melted butter and season with nutmeg and pepper to taste.

When the onions are nearly tender, remove from the heat and drain. Let them cool enough to handle and scoop out the center of each, leaving about a half-inch-thick shell. Chop enough of the scooped-out onion to make ¼ cup and stir it into the stuffing mixture. Fill the cavity of each onion with the stuffing, mounding it up if necessary. Be careful not to break the onions' outer layers that form the shell.

Lightly butter a 9-inch-square flameproof casserole and add the onions, stuffed-side up. Pour enough broth around them to come halfway up their sides and bake until the tops are golden and the stuffing is cooked through, about half an hour.

Carefully transfer the onions to shallow individual serving dishes. If you don't have a flameproof casserole, transfer the cooking liquid to a saucepan, scraping loose as much of the cooking residue in the dish as possible. If the casserole is flame-proof, put it directly over the heat. Bring the liquid to a boil over medium-high heat. Let it boil until it is reduced and beginning to get syrupy. Off the heat, whisk in the cold bits of butter a little at a time until the sauce is rich and thick enough to suit you. Pour some of the sauce over the onions, sprinkle them with parsley, and serve at once, passing the remaining sauce separately.

Prosciutto Stuffed Zucchini

Throughout the summers of my childhood, my mother's garden provided a bounty of zucchini, and she was always looking for new ways to bring that bounty to the table. Our favorite was her stuffed zucchini: cooked until they were barely done, then halved lengthwise, hollowed out, and stuffed with a savory meat filling. It was a nice surprise to find out that the idea was also a favorite of Italian cooks, particularly on the Ligurian Riviera, where stuffed vegetables are an art. This is also lovely with sweet marjoram or oregano substituted for half or all of the parsley.

SERVES 4

4 small, slender zucchini, each less than 6 inches long
3 tablespoons unsalted butter
¼ cup minced shallot or yellow onion
½ cup chopped prosciutto
2 tablespoons chopped flat-leaf (Italian) parsley
1 cup fine, soft bread crumbs
½ cup freshly grated Parmigiano-Reggiano cheese, divided
Salt and whole black pepper in a mill
Whole nutmeg in a grater

Position a rack in the upper third of the oven and preheat to 375°. Scrub the zucchini under cold running water and drain well. Put the zucchini in a lidded pan wide enough to hold them in one layer and add enough water to completely cover them, then lift out the squash, cover the pan, and bring the water to a boil.

Slip the squash back into the pan, cover, and let the water come back to a boil. Reduce the heat and simmer until they're barely tender, about 10 minutes. Drain and rinse well under cold running water. Let them cool enough to handle, split them in half lengthwise and carefully scoop out the center pulp, leaving a ¼-inch-thick shell. Roughly chop the pulp.

Put the shallots and butter in a skillet over medium heat. Sauté, tossing occasionally, until the shallots are softened, about 4 minutes. Add the pulp and cook until the liquid is evaporated. Add the prosciutto and parsley, toss until hot, and turn off the heat. Stir in the bread crumbs and half of the cheese and toss to mix. Season the filling well with salt, pepper, and nutmeg, to taste.

Divide the filling among the zucchini shells and put them in a lightly buttered casserole, stuffing-side up. Sprinkle the remaining cheese evenly over them and bake until they're hot through and their tops are golden brown, about 30 minutes.

Ham and Figs

Since southern country ham, Spanish jamón serrano and Ibérico hams, and Italian prosciutto are kissing cousins, it shouldn't be surprising that they're all used in similar ways in their respective cuisines. For example, all of them are often served with fresh seasonal fruit. As is true for most things with few ingredients, the strength of the combination of ham and fruit lies entirely in the quality of its primary components. The fruit must be perfectly ripe and the ham of the best quality—not too salty with just an undertone of sweet smokiness.

SERVES 4

---

4 large ripe figs (or 8, if they are small)

2 lemons

16 paper-thin slices raw, dry-aged country ham (preferred), prosciutto, jamón serrano, or jamón ibérico, or cooked country ham

¼ pound (1 stick or ½ cup) best-quality unsalted butter, softened (optional)

Whole black pepper in a mill

Cut the figs lengthwise into quarters and each lemon into 4 wedges.

Fold the ham slices in half and arrange them on four salad plates, folded side out and centers overlapping. Arrange the figs and lemons in an alternating pinwheel pattern on top of the ham.

If you're serving butter, whip it until fluffy and light, and put a large dollop in the center of each plate. Serve immediately, passing the peppermill separately.

Old-Fashioned Southern Ham Bone Soup

This old mixed vegetable soup can be found all over the South, its composition varying from region to region. Like any good vegetable soup, it's a bit of a paradox: regardless of where the pot is stirred and what the cook has put into it, it's best made in the summer, when all the various ingredients are in season and at peak flavor; unfortunately, it's also when the heat index is at its peak, and steaming pots and hot soup are the last thing on anyone's mind.

Fortunately, it needs very little attention once it's assembled and simmering. And as for eating it on a hot day, like most vegetable soups, this is equally as good cold (that is, a little cooler than room temperature) and makes a refreshing and cooling summer lunch or supper.

Whether it's flavoring a soup, a pot of collards or other greens, or beans and other vegetables, the broth that is the base for this soup is an indispensable element of traditional southern cooking. In the old days, it was made as needed, either from leftover ham bones and scraps or from smoked ham hocks or knuckles. For busy modern cooks, however, it's good to know that the broth can be made well ahead and frozen in small batches so that it's ready to use as needed. The amounts given here will yield about 3½ quarts of broth, more than you'll need for the soup, but it freezes well and is a good thing to have on hand.

FOR THE BROTH

1 whole ham bone, with some meat still attached,
   or 1½ pounds ham hocks
2 medium yellow onions, peeled and thinly sliced
1 medium celery stalk, thickly sliced, the leafy top left whole
1 medium carrot, peeled and thickly sliced
4 quarts water
8–10 whole black peppercorns
1 whole hot pepper such as cayenne, Serrano, or jalapeño
1 large flat-leaf (Italian) parsley sprig or 2–3 large parsley stems
2 (3-inch) thyme sprigs
1 large bay leaf
Salt

FOR THE SOUP

3 tablespoons rendered ham drippings, bacon drippings,
   or vegetable oil
1 medium yellow onion, split lengthwise, peeled, and
   diced small
1 large carrot, trimmed, peeled, and diced small
2 large celery stalks, washed, strung, and diced small,
   leafy tops reserved whole
1 small turnip, trimmed, peeled, and diced small
4 cups peeled, seeded, and diced ripe tomatoes
   (about 12 Roma or 8 large)
Salt and whole black pepper in a mill

2 cups small fresh or frozen green butterbeans (green
    lima beans)
2 cups fresh-cut (about 2–3 large ears) or frozen white
    sweet corn kernels
2 cups diced yellow crookneck squash (about 2 medium)
2 cups diced cabbage (about ½ small head)
2 cups capped and sliced fresh okra (about 8 ounces
    whole pods)
1–2 cups small-diced cooked ham, preferably from the
    ham bone used for the broth

To make the broth: Put the bone or hock, onion, celery and its leafy top, carrot, and water in an 8- to 10-quart stockpot. Bring it slowly to a simmer over medium heat, uncovered, skimming off any scum that rises. It'll take about 30 minutes. When it's simmering, add the peppercorns, hot pepper, and herbs, reduce the heat to low, and simmer slowly for at least 2 hours; if you have the time, 3–4 hours is better. (If you want to use a slow cooker and it's large enough, cook the bone or hock, onion, celery and its leafy top, carrot, and water on high until it starts to boil, about an hour; turn the heat to low, add the peppercorns, hot pepper, and herbs, and let it simmer for at least 8 hours or overnight.) Turn off the heat. Taste and add salt if needed, then let the broth cool. Strain it into a bowl, discarding the solids, and refrigerate until the fat on top has solidified. Skim off the fat and discard it or save it to use for sautéing. The fat will keep in the refrigerator for up to 2 weeks and up to 3 months if frozen in a well-sealed container. The broth will keep for up to a week, refrigerated, or freeze it in small batches for up to 3 months.

To make the soup: Warm the fat and onions in a heavy-bottomed 4- to 6-quart pot over medium heat. Sauté, stirring often, until it's translucent but not colored, 2–3 minutes. Add the carrot, celery, and turnip and sauté until beginning to soften, 2–3 minutes longer.

Add 8 cups of the broth and the tomatoes with their juice, bring this to a boil, and lower the heat to a steady simmer. Season lightly with salt and generously with pepper and let simmer for an hour.

Add the butterbeans, corn, squash, cabbage, okra, and ham and raise the heat long enough to bring the soup back to a boil, stirring often to make sure it doesn't scorch. Lower the heat once more to a steady simmer and cook until the vegetables are all very tender, 30–45 minutes. Longer won't hurt a thing. Taste and adjust the salt and pepper and simmer a moment or two longer.

Bonnie's Ham and Crab Gumbo

Most people associate gumbo with New Orleans, but its roots are African (the name even derives from an African name for okra), and it's found all over the South, especially where people of West African descent have settled, crossing all ethnic and regional boundaries. This one is the handiwork of Bonnie Gaster, a native of Tybee Island, Georgia, Savannah's official beach. There's a lot going on here, yet no one flavor dominates. Still, each is allowed to shine at its best. The secret is that while the broth is allowed to simmer for a long time, the gumbo is not, so the crab, tomatoes, and okra are tender but still fresh and sweet tasting.

SERVES ABOUT 30

FOR THE BROTH

1 large, meaty ham bone from a spiral-sliced ham
(about 4½ pounds)
6 quarts water
1 teaspoon crushed hot red pepper
2–3 leafy celery heart stalks

FOR THE GUMBO

½ cup canola or other vegetable oil
¾ cup all-purpose flour
2 large Vidalia or other sweet onions, trimmed,
split lengthwise, peeled, and chopped
3 cups thinly sliced celery
1 medium red bell pepper, stem, core, and membrane
removed, diced
1 small green bell pepper, stem, core, and membrane
removed, diced
4 large garlic cloves, lightly crushed, peeled, and minced
1 large ripe jalapeño or other hot red pepper, stem,
core and seeds removed, minced
1 large bay leaf

6 cups sliced young, tender okra, trimmed and
cut ½-inch thick
2 pounds ripe Roma tomatoes, cored, quartered
lengthwise, seeded, and sliced ½ inch thick
2 generous tablespoons seafood boiling spice
(such as Old Bay Seasoning)
2 teaspoons salt
2 tablespoons freshly cracked black pepper
1 tablespoon chopped fresh thyme
¼ cup chopped flat-leaf (Italian) parsley
5 cups shredded or diced cooked ham (from bones)
3 pounds (6 packed cups) cooked and picked crabmeat
2 cups sliced green onions, divided
8 cups cooked rice
About 30 cooked, peeled shrimp, for garnish

Pick over the ham bone and remove about 5 cups of meat. Make
the broth following the method on page 30. When it's cool,
strain and degrease it, reserving about ¼ cup of fat. You may
make the broth up to 3 or 4 days ahead. Cover and refrigerate
until needed.

To make the gumbo, warm the oil in a heavy-bottomed 10- to
12-quart stockpot or Dutch oven over medium heat. Sprinkle in
the flour and stir until smooth. Cook, stirring constantly, until
the roux is pecan-colored (light brown; a bit deeper than tan).
It should smell pleasantly toasty, not scorched. Stir in the onions
and let them wilt, about 2 minutes, then add the celery and simmer until translucent, about 2 minutes. Add both bell peppers
and let wilt, about a minute. Add the garlic, jalapeño, and bay
leaf and stir until fragrant, about a minute longer. Add the okra,
and toss until it is bright green, then add the tomatoes and let
them heat through.

Add 12 cups of ham broth, the seafood spice, salt, black pepper, thyme, and parsley. Let it come to a simmer and cook until the okra and tomatoes are just tender, about 10–15 minutes. Add the ham, let it heat through, then add the crab and 1 cup of the green onions and let the gumbo come back to a simmer. Taste and adjust the seasonings and simmer another minute to let the flavors meld. Remove the bay leaf. Serve with about ¼ cup of rice in the bottom of each bowl, garnishing each serving with a whole shrimp and the remaining green onions.

MaMa's Ham Dumplings

Every year until after I finished college, the end of the Christmas holidays was marked by my grandmother's ham dumplings. It was her way of using up what was left of the Christmas ham, but I think we almost looked forward to having those dumplings more than the meat.
The first choice of ham for dumplings is country ham, but they're even respectable made with brine-cured ham, just so long as it isn't doesn't have a sweet glaze and isn't too smoky tasting.

SERVES 6

---

6 cups ham broth (page 30)

1 cup diced or shredded cooked ham

10 ounces (about 2 cups) unbleached all-purpose flour

½ teaspoon baking soda

1 teaspoon baking powder

1 teaspoon salt

4 tablespoons lard, vegetable shortening, or unsalted butter

1 cup whole milk buttermilk or plain, all-natural whole-milk yogurt thinned to buttermilk consistency with water or milk

¼ cup chopped flat-leaf (Italian) parsley, plus 2 tablespoons for garnish

---

Bring the broth and ham to a simmer over medium heat. Sift together the flour, baking soda, baking powder, and salt into a mixing bowl. Cut in the fat with a pastry blender until the flour resembles coarse cornmeal. Make a well in the center of the dry ingredients and pour in the buttermilk. With a wooden spoon and as few strokes as possible, quickly stir the ingredients together.

Lightly flour a smooth wood or plastic laminate work surface and turn the dough out onto it. Flour your hands and gently push the dough away from you to flatten it. Fold it in half, gently press it flat with the heel of your hand, and give it a quarter turn. Repeat this until the dough is just smooth, about 12–15 folds. Dust the work surface and the dough with more flour and roll it out to ⅛ inch thick. Quickly cut it into 1-inch strips, and then cut them into 2-inch lengths.

Drop the dumplings a few at a time into the simmering broth; when they've all been added, let them simmer for 5 minutes. Stir in the parsley and simmer for 2–3 minutes more. Ladle the dumplings onto a serving platter or individual soup plates, sprinkle them with more parsley, and serve at once.

Ham and Asparagus

One of the world's great natural flavor pairings is that of sweet fresh asparagus with ham. It's so universal that this entire book might easily be filled with the many variations of the pairing. You'll find more ways to take advantage of the combination elsewhere in this book, but here are a couple of timeless classic beginnings to get us started.

Ham-Wrapped Asparagus

This is the most basic pairing of ham with asparagus. Its variations are legion: sometimes the asparagus is coated with butter, cream cheese, goat cheese, or mustard before the ham is wrapped around it, and sometimes the little bundles are baked. But when the two main ingredients are of impeccable quality, additions are overkill and cooking becomes superfluous: They need absolutely nothing to make their mating shine. In fact, when the asparagus is really fresh-cut, it doesn't even need the initial blanching that's called for here. The secret is freshness: although some cooks make ham-wrapped asparagus well ahead of serving, it loses some of its character if allowed to sit for too long once it's assembled. I always make them within an hour of serving.

Choose medium-thick spears of asparagus for this: the pencil-thin and extra-fat varieties don't work quite as well.

SERVES 4–6

---

16 medium-thick asparagus spears

1 tablespoon salt

8 paper-thin slices prosciutto, Serrano ham, or raw dry-aged country ham, well-chilled

---

Prepare a large basin of ice water. Fill a wide, deep skillet with at least 1½ inches of water. Cover and bring it to a boil over medium-high heat. Meanwhile, trim the cut end of the asparagus and peel the tough lower part of the stems. Cut off the bottoms so that the spears are uniformly 5–6 inches long. Set the trimmed and peeled bases aside for use in a soup, sauté, or pasta sauce.

Add the salt to the boiling water, slip in the asparagus spears, and let them cook until they're bright green but still firm, 1–2 minutes. Immediately drain and drop them into the ice water, gently stirring until chilled. Spread on a rimmed pan lined with linen or paper towels and refrigerate until you're ready to wrap them.

While the ham is quite cold, cut each piece lengthwise into 2 strips. Wrap a strip of it around each asparagus, spiraling it up the stem. Put each piece on a serving platter as it's wrapped. Cover the platter with damp paper towels or linen tea towels and chill until ready to serve.

Stir-Fried Ham and Asparagus with Scallions, Southern-Style

Stir-frying is mostly associated with Asia, but it really is a universal technique. In this one, the accent is southern, thanks to the combination of country ham, scallions, and a squeeze of lemon juice. It's a fine first course, side dish, or even main dish served with rice or tossed with short, tubular pasta such as penne.

SERVES 4

1¼ pounds fat-stemmed asparagus

1 tablespoon salt

3 tablespoons unsalted butter

2 ounces (⅛-inch-thick) sliced country ham or prosciutto cut into 2-inch-long strips (about ½ cup)

Salt and whole black pepper in a mill

4 small scallions, trimmed and thinly sliced

1 large lemon cut into 8 wedges

Trim off the cut end of the asparagus and peel the tough lower part with a vegetable peeler. Drop it in cold water and let it soak for a few minutes.

Prepare a large basin of ice water. Fill a wide, deep skillet with at least 1½-inches of water. Cover and bring it to a boil over medium-high heat. Add the salt and slip in the asparagus, letting it fall into the water away from you. Cook until it's bright green but still crisp, about 1–2 minutes, depending on the thickness. Immediately drain and drop it into the ice water, gently stirring until it's quite cold. Drain, pat dry, and cut it on the diagonal into 2-inch lengths.

Heat the butter in the skillet in which the asparagus was blanched over medium heat. When the butter is hot, add the ham and toss until it loses its raw red color. Add the asparagus and stir-fry until it's almost tender, about 1 minute. Season well with salt and pepper. Add the scallions and toss until they're bright green and the asparagus is done to your taste, about a minute longer. Turn off the heat, give it one last toss, and serve at once with lemon wedges.

Ham and Melon

Probably the most classic ham-and-fruit pairing is ham is with melon. It isn't really a recipe: whether the ham is jamón serrano, jamón ibérico, prosciutto di Parma, or the South's own country ham, it's simply sliced tissue-thin and wrapped around juicy-sweet wedges of cantaloupe or honeydew melon. In the South, the ham may also be cut a bit thicker, sautéed, and finished with redeye gravy (page 18) that's spooned over a wedge of the fruit for an added hot/cold contrast. Though not as well known, the combination also turns up in the soup pot.

Chilled Melon and Ham Soup

This exquisitely simple soup combines sweet, ice-cold melon with salty ham in the more traditional way. There are many versions; in some, the ham isn't cooked but is roughly torn and scattered over the top of each serving. But I love the contrast of crispy ham "bacon" against the smooth, cool melon purée. Sherry vinegar is traditionally used in combination with lime juice, but some versions use only lime juice, and you may omit the sherry vinegar if you can't get it where you live.

SERVES 4

---

1 medium ripe honeydew or cantaloupe melon

1 medium cucumber (optional)

2 tablespoons sherry vinegar (optional)

1 tablespoon fresh lime juice, or 3 tablespoons if not using vinegar, or to taste

Salt and whole white pepper in a mill

4 very thin slices Serrano ham, prosciutto, or aged country ham

¼ cup lightly packed fresh mint leaves

Cut the melon in half, seed it, cut each half into thick wedges, peel, and cut them into 1-inch chunks. If using the cucumber, peel, cut it in half, and seed it, then cut it into 1-inch chunks.

Purée the melon (and cucumber, if using) with the vinegar, if using, and lime juice in a blender and season to taste with salt and white pepper. Pour it into a bowl, cover, and chill for at least 2 hours.

Brush a nonstick pan with olive oil and warm it over medium heat. Lay a couple of slices of the ham in it and cook as for Ham Crisps (page 20) and repeat with the remaining ham.

When ready to serve, taste the soup and adjust the vinegar (or lime juice), salt, and pepper, then ladle it into chilled serving bowls. Cut the crisped ham into strips, or roughly crumble it, or break it into 2–3 large pieces. Tear the mint into small pieces or cut it into julienne strips. Scatter the mint and ham strips or crumbles over the top of each serving. Or, if using larger pieces of ham, scatter the mint and then stand 1–2 pieces of the ham up in each bowl. Serve immediately.

Chinese Winter Melon and Ham Soup

While closely related to the fruit that Westerners are accustomed to calling melons, Chinese winter melon is really a gourd and in China is eaten as a vegetable. A whole winter melon looks similar to a watermelon, but its flesh is white, and when mature, there's a chalky/waxy white bloom on its tough green skin. If you can't find it, Chinese cooking maven Helen Chen suggests using peeled watermelon rind, which makes a very nice substitute.

SERVES 4

4 Chinese black mushrooms (dried shiitake)
1 (1-pound) slice winter melon or the rind from a 2-pound piece watermelon
1 (4-ounce) thin slice country ham, trimmed of fat
4 cups ham broth (page 30) or chicken broth
1 (1-inch) chunk fresh ginger root, peeled and cut into fine julienne
4 small scallions, trimmed and thinly sliced on the diagonal

Cover the mushrooms with cold or water that's just off the boil. Soak until softened, 15–30 minutes for cold water, 5–15 minutes for hot (but let them cool before trying to handle them). Gently squeeze the mushrooms dry and thickly slice them. Reserve their liquid.

Meanwhile, peel the melon and remove the seeds and any soft connective tissue at the seeds. If using watermelon rind, peel it. Cut the flesh or rind into ½-inch cubes. You should have about 2–2½ cups. Slice the ham into very thin strips. You should have about ¾ cup.

Bring the broth and reserved mushroom soaking liquid to a boil in a heavy-bottomed 3-quart saucepan over medium-high heat. Add the melon, bring the liquid back to a boil, and lower the heat to a slow simmer. Cook until the melon is translucent and almost tender, about 20 minutes. Add the ham, ginger, and mushrooms and simmer until the ham and melon are both tender, about 10 minutes longer. Remove the soup from the heat, stir in the scallions, and serve immediately.

Ham and Eggs

Of all the things in the world's cuisines that have been paired together, there's surely nothing more universal, versatile, and soul-nourishing than the mating of ham with eggs. Whether presented in the elaborate elegance of eggs Benedict or homespun simplicity of sunny-side-up eggs nestled beside a sizzling ham steak, this culinary duo gives us strength to face the day, helps us celebrate the middle of it, and provides warming comfort at its weary end.

The lovely thing about the many variations on ham and eggs is that most of them are quite simple, but like most simple things, they require two things: first-rate ingredients and finesse from the cook.

Before you begin any of these recipes, note that the eggs must be at room temperature or they won't cook evenly. If you're taking them from the refrigerator just before cooking and don't have time to allow them to sit until they've lost their chill, put them whole (still in the shell) into a heatproof bowl, cover them with very hot tap water, and let them sit for 2 minutes. Drain well and cook immediately.

Classic American Ham and Eggs

In American Cookery, *his timeless love song to his native cooking, James Beard waxed eloquent on the virtues of ham and eggs, and recalled that there was a time in our history when one could safely order this dish at any inn or country diner in the land with certainty that it would be well made. Sadly, this is no longer true, but you can still have this glorious bit of perfection at home—and it takes only minutes to prepare.*

The eggs for this dish are usually called either fried or sunny-side-up, the latter because the yolks are still soft and runny and remain a bright, sunny yellow. "Fried" is a misleading moniker because they really don't "fry" but gently cook in barely enough fat to keep them from sticking to the pan. The fat can be the drippings from the ham, but purists like Beard insisted that they be cooked only in butter. I'll leave that entirely up to you.

If you like the eggs to be a little more done, have a teakettle of water simmering so that you'll have boiling hot water with which to baste the eggs where directed below.

SERVES 2

4 large fresh eggs
2 (6-ounce) slices cooked ham or ham steaks (preferably
   country ham), cut $1/4$–$1/2$ inch thick
2 tablespoons unsalted butter, divided
Salt and whole black pepper in a mill

If the eggs are straight from the refrigerator, warm them in their shells as directed on page 49. Trim the excess fat from the ham, but leave some of it attached.

Warm a heaping tablespoon of the fat trimmings in a heavy-bottomed 11- to 12-inch nonstick pan or well-seasoned carbon steel or cast-iron pan. Cook until the fat is rendered and remove the cracklings. Add 1 tablespoon of the butter, swirling it as it melts until the entire bottom of the pan is evenly coated.

Add the ham slices or steaks and slowly cook, turning them often, until the ham's fat is golden and crisp at its edges and the meat is lightly browned, about 8–10 minutes. Transfer to a warm platter or individual serving plates.

If using the ham drippings for the eggs, spoon off all but about a tablespoon, or leave just enough to barely cover the bottom of the pan. If using butter, pour off the drippings, wipe out the pan, and add about 1 tablespoon of the butter, swirling it until it just coats the bottom.

Break 1 egg into a small bowl or ramekin and slip it into the pan. Quickly but gently push the yolk to the center of the white with a wooden spoon, and if the white spreads a lot (a sign of an older egg) gently push the edges inward to make a neat round. Repeat with the remaining eggs. If your stove isn't level and the eggs tend to flow to one side of the pan, add the egg on the side that's lowest and then turn the pan halfway around on the burner before adding the next one. Let them gently cook until the white is just opaque and barely set, about a minute.

If you like the white to be a little more done on top or prefer the yolk a little more cooked, cover the pan with a lid or baste each egg with a spoonful of boiling water and then cover the pan. Whether covered or open, continue cooking until the white is set to your liking, about 1–1½ minutes longer. A proper fried egg should have a nicely set but still soft white, and its yolk should be a bright sunny orange-yellow and still rather runny. Season with salt and pepper to taste, and immediately transfer them to a platter or warm plates, and serve at once.

NOTES ❋ Some love a fried egg with a crispy, browned edge. To accomplish this without making the white tough, melt the fat over medium heat and let it get almost bubbling hot before adding the egg. It'll bubble and sizzle the moment it touches the pan. Quickly but gently push the yolk to the center, let it cook until the bottom of the egg is just opaque, then lower the heat and continue as above.

Ham and Eggs à la Suisse

Classic eggs à la Suisse are baked with butter, a grating of fine Gruyère or Emmentaler cheese, and a bit of cream and doesn't usually contain ham. But on a drive through Switzerland with fellow students from an architectural graduate studies program headquartered in Genoa, Italy, we stumbled on a cozy little inn that served up this filling (and best of all for tuition-impoverished wallets, cheap) version in which a few thin slices of fine old ham lined the bottom of the dish. It was so good that we made sure that the inn was in our path as we headed home.

SERVES 2

4 large eggs

2 tablespoons unsalted butter

4 thin slices French ham, prosciutto, Westphalian ham,
    or aged country ham, cut into ½-inch-wide strips

½ cup coarsely grated Gruyère or Emmentaler cheese, divided

Salt and whole black pepper in a mill

¼ cup heavy cream

Position a rack in the center of the oven and preheat to 350°. If the eggs are straight from the refrigerator, warm them in their shells as directed on page 49. Put a tablespoon each of the butter in two small (preferably 5-inch round) gratin dishes, put the dishes on a rimmed baking sheet, and heat them in the oven for 5 minutes.

Remove the dishes from the oven, and, holding them with a pot holder or thick towel, swirl until the melted butter is evenly spread over the bottom of the dish. Divide the ham evenly between them, scattering it evenly over the bottom. Sprinkle 1 tablespoon of the cheese over the ham in each dish.

One at a time, break the eggs into a small bowl or ramekin and slip them over the ham, 2 per dish. Season them with salt and pepper, then scatter the remaining cheese evenly over them. Drizzle the cream evenly over the eggs and bake until the eggs are set, about 8 minutes.

Prosciutto and Eggs

Italian cookery maven Michele Scicolone was first introduced to the heady pairing of prosciutto and eggs in Montepulciano, a village in Tuscany. Like most really good Italian cooking, this is exquisitely simple yet perfectly balanced in its flavors.

SERVES 2

4 large eggs
1 tablespoon unsalted butter
4–6 thinly sliced imported Italian prosciutto
Salt and whole black pepper in a mill

If the eggs are straight from the refrigerator, warm them in their shells as directed on page 49. Melt the butter in a 9- to 10-inch nonstick or well-seasoned cast-iron or carbon steel skillet over medium-low heat. Carefully and completely cover the bottom of the pan with the prosciutto, overlapping it slightly.

One at a time, break the eggs into a small bowl or ramekin and slip them onto the prosciutto. Season lightly with salt and pepper, and cook gently until the egg whites are completely opaque, about 1 minute.

Cover the pan and continue cooking until the eggs are set and done to your taste, 1–2 minutes longer. Serve immediately.

Omelettes and Frittate

Among the very best dishes in which ham and eggs come together is the classic French omelette and Italian frittata. They may, on the surface of things, seem to be close cousins; indeed, frittate are often even called open-faced Italian omelettes in America. But actually just about the only things these two dishes have in common are eggs and butter. The techniques involved are nothing alike, nor are the final products that each technique produces. A proper French omelette is soft, fluffy, and slightly runny at its center. Cooked over lively heat, an omelette is kept constantly moving in the pan so that the eggs set in soft curds, and is finished by being rolled over on itself onto the serving plate to form a neat oval. A frittata, on the other hand, is flat, round, and firm. It cooks on both sides over low heat and isn't touched except to expose its top side to direct heat. When finished, it's served by cutting the flat round into wedges, like a pizza.

Omelette au Jambon et Fromage (Ham and Cheese Omelette)

If you have trouble with the swirling technique given here, just stir the eggs with a fork while gently shaking the pan back and forth, making sure that the tines of the fork never touch the bottom of the pan.

SERVES 1

2–3 large very fresh eggs
2 tablespoons unsalted butter, divided, plus more for glazing
2 tablespoons diced cooked ham, preferably country ham or
   French ham, or thick-cut and diced prosciutto
Salt and whole black pepper in a mill
2 tablespoons grated Gruyère cheese

If the eggs are straight from the refrigerator, warm them in their shells as directed on page 49. Put ½ tablespoon of the butter in a small skillet over medium heat. When it's melted, add the ham and gently sauté until it's heated through. Remove from the heat but keep it warm.

Break the eggs into a mixing bowl. Season them lightly with salt and pepper and beat with a fork (not a whisk) until the yolks and whites are well mixed but not foaming—about 40 strokes.

Put the remaining butter in a well-seasoned 9- to 10-inch omelette or nonstick pan and turn on the heat to medium high. When butter stops foaming and sizzling, the pan is ready. Give the eggs 4 to 5 more strokes with the fork and pour them into the pan, gently shaking the pan with your other hand. Let them set for 10–15 seconds.

Begin shaking the pan in a circular motion so that the eggs never settle on the bottom of the pan but are always moving: after 5–10 seconds, if there seems to be an excess of runny egg around the edges, lift the edges of the eggs with a fork and let the excess egg flow underneath (a three-egg omelette sometimes will need this step). Never stop moving the pan. A soft, slightly runny omelette is ready after 10–20 seconds longer; a solid but still moist omelette is ready after 20–30 seconds.

Sprinkle the cheese over the entire surface, then tip the pan and flip ⅓ of the omelette over on itself. Sprinkle the ham down the center and, using a fork or spatula, or by firmly tapping the handle of the pan, let the omelette slide into the pan's outer curving edge.

Hold a serving plate in your free hand at 45 degrees. With the side of the pan where the omelette rests against the plate, tip the pan up and let the omelette fold over onto itself onto the plate. Tuck its edges into a neat oval, quickly rub the surface with a little butter, and serve immediately.

Frittata con Prosciutto e Formaggio (Ham and Cheese Frittata)

The classic technique for cooking both sides of a frittata is to flip it once the bottom is set, which some Italians do by theatrically tossing it into the air just as short-order cooks flip pancakes. A safer way is to slide the partially cooked frittata onto a plate and then invert it over the pan. Still another, much easier way is to simply slide the pan under a preheated broiler. The frittata will puff up under the broiler (which it does not do when fully cooked on the stovetop), but don't worry: it will begin deflating as soon as it comes out of the oven. Classically, a frittata should be colored the palest gold, but I actually like it to be a little browned. Just be careful not to let it brown too much: if it does, the surface will be tough and the center dry and dull.

While many recipes conclude with the words "serve at once," frittate do not because they can be served as soon as they come from the pan but are just as nice served barely warm or at room temperature. Frittate should never be refrigerated since they lose their appeal after they're stone cold, so make them within a couple of hours of serving them.

SERVES 4 AS A MAIN DISH

6 large fresh eggs

Salt and whole black pepper in a mill

2 tablespoons unsalted butter

½ cup thinly sliced prosciutto, cut into thin strips

1 tablespoon chopped fresh sage or flat-leaf (Italian) parsley

¾ cup coarsely grated Parmigiano-Reggiano cheese, divided

Position a rack about 8 inches below the heat source and preheat the broiler for at least 15 minutes. If the eggs are straight from the refrigerator, warm them in their shells as directed on page 49. Break the eggs into a mixing bowl and lightly beat to mix, season well with salt and pepper, and beat until smooth.

Melt the butter in a heavy-bottomed 10-inch nonstick or well-seasoned pan over medium heat. When the butter is foaming, swirl the pan to evenly coat it. Stir the prosciutto, sage or parsley, and ½ cup of the Parmigiano into the eggs, then pour the eggs into the pan, stirring in the bowl as you pour to keep the ham and cheese evenly mixed in. Reduce the heat to low and cook until the bottom is set and only the top is wet. Turn off the heat.

Sprinkle the remaining Parmigiano over the top of the frittata, put the pan under the broiler, and broil until the top is set, about 1 minute. Serve hot, warm, or at room temperature.

Ham Salads, Biscuits, and Sandwiches

Though John Montagu, the fourth Earl of Sandwich, is often given credit for having "invented" the sandwich so he could eat supper with one hand and keep playing cards with the other, it needs to be pointed out that he most definitely did no such thing. The idea of encasing meat in bread or pastry is ancient, possibly as old as bread itself. Still, he probably did popularize the idea, and it's almost certainly from his title that we get our name for two pieces of bread encasing a filling.

Although that filling doesn't have to be ham or, for that matter, any meat, no other sandwich filling provides us with as many possibilities. There's the elegantly simple tea sandwich, with its thinly sliced pieces of firm, fine-crumbed bread, spread with butter and filled with wafer-thin slices of fine baked ham or a smear of deviled ham; there's the hot, fluffy ham biscuit, that quintessential southern bread, stuffed with sautéed medallions of country ham or shavings of baked ham; there's the fat deli sandwich, piled high with boiled ham and slivers of Swiss cheese.

But the ultimate and arguably the best of all ham sandwiches is the one in which the ham is brought together with cheese between two thick, crusty slabs of bread that are then toasted until both sides are golden brown, the ham is hot, and the cheese is melted and irresistibly gooey.

Deviled Ham

The traditional southern way to eat deviled ham (also called ham paste) was to spread on a beaten biscuit, but today it's served as a spread for sandwiches, canapés, or hot buttermilk biscuits (page 75). It also makes a great cocktail appetizer with toast points or crackers.

MAKES 1½ CUPS, SERVING ABOUT 20

---

2 cups roughly chopped cooked ham, preferably country ham
1–2 tablespoons bourbon or brandy
1 cup best-quality unsalted butter, softened
Whole black pepper in a mill
Ground cayenne pepper
Whole nutmeg in a grater
About ¼ cup clarified butter, melted (enough to completely
   cover the top of the spread, optional)

Put the ham in the bowl of the food processor fitted with the steel blade and pulse until ground fine. Add a tablespoon of the bourbon or brandy and the butter and process until it's a smooth paste. Season to taste with pepper, cayenne, and nutmeg. Pulse to mix, taste, and adjust the bourbon and spices.

Press the paste into a clean crock, glass jar, or other storage container. For a traditional finish, completely cover it with clarified butter. Cover tightly and refrigerate until needed.

To serve, let it soften at room temperature for at least half an hour, or until it's spreadable.

Ham Salad I: Spread for Sandwiches or Canapés

Used as a spread for both hearty lunch-box and dainty tea sandwiches, ham salad is also a great canapé spread for soft bread rounds, crostini, or crackers. Canapés can be garnished with capers, sprigs of dill, parsley, or thinly sliced cornichon pickles. You can also scoop it into hollowed-out tomatoes or cupped lettuce leaves as a light luncheon or supper main dish. Or just pile it into a serving bowl, surround it with toast rounds or crackers, and let your company do the work. Some traditional cooks mix in chopped boiled egg. Allow 2 large hard-cooked eggs, peeled and chopped.

MAKES ABOUT 3 TO 3 ½ CUPS, SERVING 6–8

1 pound cooked lean ham
½ cup finely chopped celery
½ cup finely minced shallot or red onion or
   ½ cup finely chopped scallions
¼ cup (or to taste) finely chopped bread-and-butter
   or other sweet pickles or sweet pickle relish
1 tablespoon Dijon- or deli-style mustard
About ½ cup mayonnaise
Whole black pepper in a mill

Trim the ham of any fat or tough connective tissue and cut it into ½-inch dice. You should have about 3 cups. Put it in the bowl of a food processor fitted with a steel blade and pulse until it's coarsely but evenly chopped. If you want it for a cocktail spread, keep pulsing until it's finely ground.

Turn the ham into a mixing bowl and mix in the celery; shallots, onions or scallions; pickles or relish, and mustard. Fold in the mayonnaise until the salad is a nice spreading consistency and season with a liberal grinding of pepper. Taste and adjust the pepper and add more pickle or relish, if needed. Cover and refrigerate until needed. It will keep, well-covered and refrigerated, for up to 4 days.

Ham Salad II:
Composed Main Dish Salad

The way this salad is traditionally served in the South is similar to that of a classic French salade composé, *mounded on a bed of lettuce with its accompaniments artfully arranged around it. Another way to serve it that was once popular for fancy ladies' luncheons is to pile it into hollowed-out ripe tomatoes. Slice a little off the bottom of 4–6 ripe tomatoes so that they sit flat, cut off their tops, hollow them out with a melon baller, and fill them with the salad, mounding it on top. Serve them on a lettuce leaf, with the eggs either used as a garnish or diced and folded into the salad.*

SERVES 4–6

2½ cups diced lean cooked ham

½ cup small-diced celery

½ cup thinly sliced scallions, both white and green parts,
   or ⅓ cup finely chopped sweet onion

½ cup small-diced bread-and-butter or other sweet pickles
   (don't use relish)

1–2 tablespoons Dijon- or deli-style mustard, or to taste

About ½ cup mayonnaise

Whole black pepper in a mill

Ground cayenne or hot sauce (optional)

About 4 cups Bibb, baby romaine, or other small-leaf lettuce

2–3 ripe tomatoes, sliced

4 hard-cooked eggs, peeled and halved or quartered

½ cup whole pitted brine-cured black olives (such as Greek,
   Kalamata, or Niçoise) or green olives without a pimiento
   stuffing

12–18 small pickled okra pods (optional)

¼ cup minced flat-leaf (Italian) parsley

6 slices firm white or whole-wheat bread

Salted butter, softened

Combine the ham, celery, scallions or onions, pickles, and mustard. Fold in enough mayonnaise to bind it together. Add a liberal grinding of pepper and, if using, a pinch of cayenne or dash of hot sauce. Taste and adjust the pepper and cayenne. Cover and refrigerate for at least 2 hours. It can be made to this point up to 2 days ahead.

When ready to serve, position an oven rack 6 inches below the broiler and preheat the broiler. Cut the bread in half on the diagonal, making two triangles, and lay them on a broiler-safe rimmed baking sheet. Spread the lettuce on a serving platter and pile the ham salad in the center. Arrange the tomatoes, eggs, olives, and pickled okra, if using, around the ham salad and generously sprinkle everything with parsley. Alternatively, divide everything among 4–6 chilled salad plates and arrange the salad and accompaniments in the same way.

Toast the bread under the broiler until the tops are browned; turn it over and toast until the second side is firm but not colored. Remove it from the oven, lightly spread the tops with butter, and broil until lightly browned and crisp. Serve the salad immediately while the buttered toast is still hot.

Ham and Potato Salad

When someone dies down South, neighbors bring food to the bereaved family by the truckload. The selection will vary from town to town, but one can always count on two things: cold baked ham and potato salad. It was just a matter of time, then, before they turned up in the same bowl. Though this salad can be part of a buffet spread, it really is a main dish and is at its best served on a bed of lettuce with sliced ripe tomatoes and cheese straws, hot biscuits, or hot buttered toast on the side.

Many southerners use sweet pickles or sweet pickle relish in potato salad, and they're a nice foil for the ham in this one. If that appeals to you, substitute ½–¾ cup of small-diced bread-and-butter or other sweet pickles or sweet pickle relish for the olives.

SERVES 4–6

1¼ pounds small new red potatoes
Salt
2–4 tablespoons dry white vermouth or dry white wine
   (see Note)
1 pound cooked ham, cut into ½-inch dice (about 2 cups)
½ cup thinly sliced scallions or other green onions, both
   white and green parts
½ cup strung and chopped celery
½ cup pitted and sliced Greek black olives or ½ cup sliced
   pimiento-stuffed green olives, or a mixture of the two
2 tablespoons nonpareil capers, drained
Whole black pepper in a mill
½ cup mayonnaise
½ cup sour cream
1 tablespoon Dijon-style mustard
2 tablespoons chopped flat-leaf (Italian) parsley or dill
   for garnish

Scrub the potatoes under cold running water and cut them into 1-inch chunks. Put them in a 3-quart saucepan with enough water to completely cover them. Lightly salt them and bring to a boil over medium-high heat. Adjust the heat to a simmer, loosely cover, and cook until the potatoes are tender, about 8 minutes. Drain thoroughly and transfer them to a large bowl. Sprinkle lightly with the vermouth or wine, gently toss, and let cool.

Add the ham, scallions, celery, olives, and capers to the potatoes. Season lightly with pepper and gently toss to mix. In a separate bowl, whisk together the mayonnaise, sour cream, and mustard. Gently fold it into the salad until everything is evenly coated. Taste and adjust the salt and pepper, cover, and refrigerate for at least 2 hours. Just before serving, garnish with parsley or dill.

NOTE ❋ Dry white wine is a common ingredient in many cuisines. Unhappily it doesn't keep well once it's opened. Since we don't drink a lot of white wine in my house, I got into the habit of using dry white vermouth instead, since vermouth is a reinforced wine that keeps for a very long time once it's opened.

"Country Ham" Rolls

A traditional southern luxury that's vanishing faster than snow in June is warm baked country ham, shaved wafer-thin and piled high in biscuits or yeast rolls. Few families today are large enough to have a whole baked ham on hand, and fewer and fewer market delis offer cooked country ham thinly sliced to order. Fortunately, prosciutto is just country ham with an Italian accent and nowadays is readily available. When wafer-thin slices of prosciutto are warmed through in a skillet and then stuffed into hot biscuits or rolls, it becomes a more than acceptable substitute for those baked country hams of the old days.

These are a quick Sunday morning luxury in my house. Yes, they're made with frozen Parker House rolls. You can make your own rolls if you really want to, but when a process is already done for you, and done well, why fight it?

SERVES 6–8

1 package frozen Parker House rolls, thawed overnight
    in the refrigerator
Unsalted butter
6–8 ounces thinly sliced prosciutto

Position a rack in the center of the oven and preheat to 350°. Put the pan of rolls on a rimmed baking sheet and bake, uncovered, for about 20 minutes, or until golden brown. Turn them out of the pan and when cooled just enough to handle, split each roll, leaving one side of it attached, and if you like lightly butter them. Cover and keep warm.

Rub a little butter on the center of a nonstick or well-seasoned cast-iron pan and warm it over medium-low heat. One piece at a time, lay a slice of prosciutto on the pan and as soon as it starts to bubble (this is almost immediate), quickly fold it over 3–4 times with a pair of wooden or nylon-tipped tongs and stuff it into a prepared roll. Keep the stuffed rolls warm while repeating with the remaining ham and rolls.

Serve immediately while still warm or let them cool, return them to the pan in which the rolls were baked, and cover tightly with foil. If you're making them more than 2–3 hours ahead, refrigerate them until half an hour before you plan to serve them. When ready to serve, reheat (still tightly covered) for 5–7 minutes in a 350° oven.

Classic Southern Ham-Stuffed Buttermilk Biscuits

From at least the beginning of the nineteenth century until the middle of the twentieth, biscuits were standard breakfast fare in most southern households. They were never served at dinner, and were rarely seen at any other meal. Unless, that is, they were stuffed with ham: then they were fit for just about any setting from the tea table to the picnic hamper. This is one time when the bread around the ham is more important than the ham itself. If the biscuits aren't good, even the best of hams won't save them.

While making good biscuits isn't complicated, they do take practice. But once you get the knack, they're actually easy, and serving homemade biscuits always makes people think you've gone to a lot more trouble than you have. A lot has been written about using only a southern flour made from soft winter wheat for biscuits, and it does help ensure success, especially for a novice, but with care, you can get fine results using a good-quality all-purpose flour (a blend of soft and hard wheat flours). Because soft winter wheat (the grain used for pastry flour) has less gluten, it's more forgiving if the dough should happen to be overworked. But the real secret to good biscuits lies in not overhandling the dough.

2 cups southern soft wheat flour or soft wheat pastry flour
2 teaspoons baking powder
1 teaspoon salt
4 tablespoons chilled lard or shortening, cut into small bits
¾–1 cup whole-milk buttermilk or plain whole-milk yogurt
    thinned with milk to buttermilk consistency
About ¼ cup milk or 3–4 tablespoons melted unsalted butter,
    for brushing dough (optional)
1 recipe Sautéed Southern Country Ham (page 18, not made
    ahead but when indicated below) or ½ pound warm thinly
    sliced cooked country or regular ham

Position a rack in the center of the oven and preheat to 500°.
Sift the flour, baking powder, and salt into a mixing bowl, or put
them into the bowl and whisk to mix them. Cut in the lard or
shortening with a pastry blender until the mixture resembles
grits or polenta meal with pea-sized lumps. Do not overblend;
the small lumps of fat are what will make the biscuits flaky.

Make a well in the center and pour in ¾ cup of the buttermilk. Mix with as few strokes as possible until the dough clumps
together and pulls away from the sides of the bowl, adding milk
by the spoonful until the dough is no longer crumbly.

Turn the dough out onto a lightly floured work surface and
pat it out to 1 inch thick. Fold the dough in half and pat flat
again. Repeat twice more, then lightly flour the surface and roll
the dough out to ½–¾ inch thick.

Dip a 2-inch biscuit cutter in flour and cut the dough straight down—without twisting. Repeat until all the dough is cut, making sure that there is a cut side on all sides of each biscuit, laying each one on an ungreased baking sheet as you go; for very light, fluffy biscuits with soft edges, let them touch; for crisper biscuits (the kind I prefer), space them at least half an inch apart. Rework the leftover scraps by lightly gathering them into a lump. Gently pat and fold the dough twice more, just until the scraps hold together. Continue as instructed above. To help the tops brown, you may brush the biscuits with milk or butter. Bake until the biscuits have risen and are golden brown on top, 8–10 minutes.

While the biscuits bake, prepare the ham. As soon as the biscuits are done and barely cooled enough to handle, gently tear them in half. If you like, spread the insides with a little butter, then stuff them with the ham. To serve them warm (when they're at their best), pile them on a warm platter or into a linen-lined bread basket and serve immediately.

NOTE ❋ Though they won't be as good, the biscuits can be made and stuffed ahead. Once assembled, place them on a rimmed baking pan, allow them to cool, then cover them tightly with foil. They can be served at room temperature within a couple of hours or reheated. To reheat: about half an hour before serving, position a rack in the center of the oven and preheat to 400°. Put the pan, still well-covered with foil, into the oven to reheat for 5–6 minutes. Serve hot.

Grilled Ham and Cheese

Ham and cheese are the Ginger Rogers and Fred Astaire of the sandwich world: it's probably stretching things to say they were made for one another, but when they're brought together, magic inevitably happens. And never more so than when the ham and cheese are cozied up to one another between bread that's toasted on a hot griddle. Even when one or all of the elements—the bread, the ham, and the cheese—are in themselves ordinary, if the sandwich is well-grilled, it'll shine.

Monte Cristo

*Somewhere between monsieur (page 86) and madame (page 88)
is the monte cristo (not to be mistaken for the count of), which,
instead of being topped by an egg, is enrobed in egg batter and
pan-fried. Think of it as French toast with an attitude. Since a
monte cristo is sometimes served with a bit of sweet jam on the
side, there's no reason not to serve it as you would French toast,
with a pitcher of maple or blueberry syrup passed separately.*

SERVES 2

---

2 large eggs

¼ cup whole milk

Salt and whole white pepper in a mill

Whole nutmeg in a grater

Dijon- or deli-style brown mustard

4 thin slices firm, home-style sandwich bread
(crusts removed if desired)

Enough thinly sliced cooked ham to make three layers
in each sandwich

Enough thinly sliced Comté, Gruyère, or aged Edom cheese
to fill each sandwich in one layer

4 tablespoons clarified butter (preferred) or unsalted butter

---

Whisk together the eggs and milk in a wide, shallow bowl. Season well with salt, white pepper, and nutmeg. Spread one side of two slices of the bread thinly with mustard. Top the mustard side with three layers of ham and cover it with a layer of cheese. Cover with the remaining bread.

Warm the butter in a large, heavy-bottomed, well-seasoned cast-iron or nonstick skillet over medium-low heat. When it's hot, quickly dip a sandwich in the egg batter, turning to coat both sides, let the excess flow back into the bowl, and slip it into the pan. Repeat with the other sandwich. Raise the heat to medium and cook until the bottoms are nicely browned, about 3 minutes. Turn them over and cook until the second side is golden brown and the cheese is melted, about 3 minutes longer. Transfer them to a cutting board, cut them in half, and serve at once.

Prosciutto and Fontina Panini

Italian cooking authority Michele Scicolone tells us that what sets Italy's grilled ham and cheese sandwich apart from its cousins in other countries is that it's thin and its fillings are spare. But then a panini is really all about the quality of the ingredients, and when those ingredients are first-rate, a little of them goes a very long way.

You can prepare a panini with an electric sandwich grill/press, a grill pan fitted with a ribbed panini press, or simply a heavy-bottomed skillet. Just be sure it's thoroughly preheated before adding the sandwiches.

SERVES 2

---

4 (1/2-inch-thick) slices crusty country-style bread
1 1/2 tablespoons unsalted butter, softened
4 thin slices imported Italian prosciutto (preferably
  prosciutto di Parma)
Enough thinly sliced imported Italian Fontina cheese
  (no substitutes) to fill each sandwich in one layer
Whole black pepper in a mill
4–6 fresh sage or basil leaves (optional)
About 1 tablespoon melted butter or extra-virgin olive oil,
  for grilling

Spread one side of all 4 slices of the bread with butter. Cover the buttered side of two of them with the prosciutto and then enough fontina to cover them in one layer. Sprinkle the cheese with a very light grinding of pepper and, if you like, top with 2–3 whole sage or basil leaves. Cover with the remaining bread, buttered-side in.

If using a grill/press, preheat it to medium heat. If using a grill pan and press or skillet, heat for 3–4 minutes over medium heat (heating the press separately from the grill pan). Lightly brush one side of the sandwiches with half the melted butter or oil and lay them on the grill/press, grill pan, or skillet, then brush their tops with the remaining butter or oil.

If using a grill/press, close it and grill until the sandwiches are toasted and the cheese is melted and hot, about 3–4 minutes. If using a grill pan and press, put the heated press on top of the sandwiches and cook until toasted and hot, also about 3–4 minutes. If using a skillet, weight the sandwiches with a second, smaller skillet or just press them down with the back of a spatula. Cook until the bottoms are toasted, about 3 minutes; turn the sandwiches over and cook, again weighting them with the skillet or pressing them with the spatula, until that side is toasted and the cheese is melted and hot, about 2–3 minutes longer. Serve immediately.

Grilled Ham and Pimiento Cheese

Given all the variations on the Croque Monsieur (page 86), it might be tempting to dub this a "Croque Belle," since any southern hostess worth her y'all keeps good pimiento cheese on hand at all times. But let's not. Sometimes called "the house pâté of the South," pimiento cheese, when sensibly made, is a carefully balanced triad of good sharp cheddar cheese, mayonnaise, and diced pimientos from a jar—yes, from a jar. It makes a stellar grilled cheese sandwich, and when you tuck in a little good ham, why, that sandwich goes straight over the top.

Down South, all you have to do to start one of the biggest fights you've ever seen is to mention sugar in cornbread or recite your pimiento cheese recipe followed by a pronouncement that it's the only way to make it. The one included here is my only way.

SERVES 2

FOR THE PIMIENTO CHEESE (MAKES ABOUT 2 1/2 CUPS)
8 ounces extra-sharp cheddar cheese
2 ounces Parmigiano-Reggiano cheese
5–6 generous tablespoons mayonnaise, or to taste
1 (4-ounce) jar diced pimientos, drained but liquid reserved,
    roughly chopped
Ground cayenne pepper
Dry English mustard

FOR THE SANDWICHES
4 slices firm, home-style sandwich bread
Enough thinly sliced deli ham, prosciutto, or cooked country
    ham to make two layers in each sandwich
Deli- or Dijon-style mustard (optional)
About 2 tablespoons unsalted butter, softened

To make the pimiento cheese, coarsely grate the cheddar with a box grater and finely grate the Parmigiano, using the finest holes of the grater or a rotary cheese grater. Mix them together. Put half the cheese into a mixing bowl and, by hand, knead in 4 tablespoons of mayonnaise until the mixture is creamy and fairly smooth. Work in the remaining cheese and pimientos, adding a tablespoon of the reserved liquid, a dash of cayenne, and a tiny pinch of dry mustard. Mix well, adding mayonnaise by tablespoons until the mixture is just spreadable but still quite thick. Taste and adjust the cayenne and mix well. Cover and refrigerate until needed.

When ready to grill the sandwiches, spread one side of two slices of the bread thickly with pimiento cheese, leaving a border about ¼-inch-wide on all sides. Top the cheese with the ham. Lightly spread one side of the remaining two slices of bread with mustard, if using, and put them on top of the ham, spread-side down.

Heat a sandwich grill/press or heat a heavy-bottomed skillet over medium heat. Spread one side of the sandwiches with butter and put them on the grill/press or pan, buttered-side down. Lightly spread the tops with butter. Close the grill and cook until the sandwiches are toasted and brown and the cheese is hot and oozing, about 3–4 minutes, or loosely cover the skillet (so that steam doesn't build up) and cook until the bottoms are toasted, about 3 minutes; turn the sandwiches over and cook until both sides are equally browned and the cheese is hot and oozing, about 3 minutes more.

Cubano
(the Classic Cuban Sandwich)

Romance novelists thrive on the notion of love at first sight. As appealing as the idea may seem, however, in real life the phenomenon is as rare as it is popular. Love at first bite, on the other hand, is something we've all experienced—that transcendent moment when a new taste touches our tongue and fires our imagination. One such moment for me was on a warm, sunny South Florida day in January of 1981. The place was La Grenada, a dim hole-in-the-wall Cuban restaurant in West Palm Beach, and the bite, my first Cubano sandwich.

In those days, Cubanos were rarely found in the South outside of Florida, but today, they've entered mainstream American cooking and have a fixed place in our food culture. Ideally, they are made with Cuban-style roasted pork that has first been infused with a spicy, bitter-orange and garlic marinade, and with Cuban bread, a long loaf that looks like an oversized baguette with a single slit down its center. If Cuban bread isn't available in your area, a loaf of French bread (not a slender baguette) or hoagie roll can be substituted.

SERVES 2

1 (12-inch-long) piece Cuban bread
Dijonstyle mustard
4 ounces thinly sliced boiled ham, preferably dry-salt-
    cured ham such as country ham or prosciutto cotto
    (Italian boiled ham)
8 ounces thinly sliced roasted pork
4 ounces deli-sliced baby Swiss cheese
4 thin slices garlic dill pickle
Rendered pork drippings or unsalted butter

Split the bread in half horizontally, leaving one side still attached. Spread each side thinly with mustard. Spread the ham evenly over the bottom side of bread. Top with the pork, cheese, and pickles. Close the sandwich and lightly press it together.

Heat a sandwich press or two iron skillets (one a little smaller than the other) or an iron bacon press and skillet over medium heat until quite hot. If you don't have a press or skillet large enough to hold the whole sandwich, cut the sandwich in half.

Brush both sides of the sandwich with the drippings or butter and grill it in the sandwich press or put it into the larger skillet and put the second heated skillet or press on top. Lightly press down. Cook, turning it over halfway through if using a skillet, until the bread is browned and crisp, the filling is hot, and the cheese is melted. Cut it in half, then cut each side in half on the diagonal. Serve hot.

Croque Monsieur

One of the most celebrated of all grilled ham and cheese sandwiches originally wasn't really grilled: the classic French quick-bite called a croque monsieur *("gentleman's munch") is classically pan-fried in butter. Since the sandwich was once served in practically every café and bar and offered by most street vendors in Paris, you'd think there would be one way to make it. There isn't.*

While some maintain that a proper croque monsieur must be pan-fried in butter, today they're often toasted on a griddle or in a sandwich grill/press. In some cafés, they're topped with béchamel sauce and sometimes grated cheese and finished in a hot oven or under a broiler.

At one time, most Parisians spread béchamel on the inside of the sandwich, and some coated the outside with the sauce before pan-frying it. But béchamel was never actually a universal component, and isn't mentioned in older editions of the French culinary encyclopedia Larousse Gastronomique. *Today, the béchamel is often omitted, but all you've really got then is a grilled ham and cheese with a fancy name.*

For some aficionados, the only bread to use for a croque monsieur is a fine-crumbed brioche (an egg-enriched, slightly sweet bread) with its crusts removed. It can, of course, be made with any firm home-style sandwich bread and the dainty crust-trimming can be omitted.

SERVES 2

---

1 tablespoon unsalted butter
1½ tablespoons instant-blending or all-purpose flour
1 cup whole milk, warmed
Salt and whole white pepper in a mill
Whole nutmeg in a grater

**4 thin slices firm, home-style sandwich bread (crusts removed
if desired)**

**Enough thinly sliced cooked French, Black Forest, or country
ham to make two layers in each sandwich**

**Enough thinly sliced Comté, Gruyère, or aged Edom cheese
to fill each sandwich in one layer**

**3 tablespoons clarified butter (preferred) or unsalted butter,
melted**

If you aren't using an electric sandwich grill/press, choose a
large, heavy-bottomed, broiler-safe nonstick or well-seasoned
cast-iron skillet. If you're finishing the sandwiches under the
broiler, position a rack 6 inches from the heat source and preheat it for at least 15 minutes.

Melt the tablespoon of unsalted butter in a small saucepan
over medium heat. Whisk in the flour until smooth. When it's
bubbly, slowly whisk in the milk and bring to a simmer, whisk-
ing constantly. Simmer until thick and no longer pasty-tasting,
about 4–5 minutes. Season to taste with salt, white pepper, and
nutmeg. Remove it from the heat but keep it warm.

Preheat the grill/press or skillet over medium heat. Spread
a little of the sauce on one side of all 4 pieces of bread as you
would mayonnaise or sandwich spread. Lay enough cheese
over the sauce on two pieces of bread to completely cover them
in one layer. Lay enough ham on the other two pieces to cover
them in two layers. Lay the cheese-covered pieces on top of the
ham, cheese-side down.

Brush the grill/press or pan with half of the melted butter
and put in the sandwiches. Brush the top sides with butter. If
you're using a grill/press, close and grill until the sandwiches
are toasted on both sides, about 3–4 minutes. If you're using an
open skillet, loosely cover it so that steam won't build up; cook

until the bottom of the sandwiches are well-toasted and the cheese is beginning to melt, about 3–4 minutes, then flip them over, again loosely cover, and toast the second side, about 2–3 minutes longer.

If you're finishing the sandwiches in the oven, spread the tops with a thin layer of béchamel and broil until the sauce is browned, 1–2 minutes. Let them settle for 2–3 minutes before serving.

VARIATION WITH BÉCHAMEL COATING ❋ If you opt to coat the outside of the sandwiches with béchamel before grilling them, choose a well-seasoned or nonstick grill/press or skillet. Spread the tops of each sandwich thinly with béchamel, then lay them on the buttered griddle/press or skillet, sauce-side down, then spread the face-up side with sauce. If using a press, brush the top half of the press with butter and close it. If using the skillet, slip the sandwiches out of the pan after the bottom is toasted, brush the pan with more butter, then return the sandwiches to the pan top-side down and toast until browned.

VARIATION ❋ Croque madame: There are many popular (and unlikely) tales about the origin of the name, but the real reason an egg-topped grilled ham and cheese is feminine is lost to time. To make it, prepare the Croque Monsieur recipe above, if you like, spread the inside of two of the pieces of bread with a bit of Dijon-style mustard before adding the béchamel. Finish them in the oven as directed in the last step, transfer to warm serving plates, and return the pan to medium heat. Add 2 tablespoons of butter and when it's hot but not browning, break an egg into a small bowl and slip it into the pan. Repeat with a second egg; cook without turning until they're opaque, then cover the pan for 1–2 minutes until the eggs are done to your taste. The yolk should still be soft and runny. Season with salt and pepper, lay them over the sandwiches, and serve at once.

Ham and Pasta

As little as twenty years ago, if you'd said the words "southern pasta" to anyone from the South (or, for that matter, from outside it), they would've looked at you as if you had two heads. We did not have anything called "pasta"; that was Italian food. What we had was called macaroni, noodles, and spaghetti—that last having an air of the exotic about it. And what we did with those things after they were boiled almost to mush resembled Italian cooking about as much as turkey "ham" resembles the real thing. To have included "pasta" in a southern cookbook would therefore have been pretentious, if not downright silly. But today, pasta—both the word itself and dozens of varieties of it beyond elbow macaroni and spaghetti—have become an integral part of our cooking, and while we've adapted to cooking the pasta al dente (firm to the bite), along with many distinctly Italian sauces for the stuff, our ways with it, even when we're indulging in a decidedly Italian dish, have taken on a distinctly southern accent.

One of the ways that our version of pasta is most like the Italians' is when we pair it with ham. That seems pretty obvious since aged, air-dried prosciutto is kissing cousin to our old country hams. But Italian cooks also mate pasta with *cotto prosciutto*, which is essentially an unsmoked version of our boiled ham. There are actually many pasta sauces in both cuisines in which the milder, more delicate flavor of boiled ham is preferable.

Ham and Macaroni Pie or Casserole

Casseroles of elbow macaroni laced with grated sharp cheddar cheese and set in egg custard (also known as macaroni and cheese and macaroni pie) are quintessential southern comfort food. In some places, they're topped with cracker or bread crumbs, but in others the topping may simply be a sprinkling of grated cheddar or dusting of black pepper. Often, they're studded with ham and, sometimes, when the cook has taken a notion to be fancy, thawed frozen green peas. I like to also add half a cup of thinly sliced scallions to brighten the flavor.

SERVES 6

Salt

1 pound elbow macaroni

8 ounces (2 cups) coarsely grated extra-sharp cheddar cheese

1½–2 cups small-diced cooked ham

Whole black pepper in a mill

4 large eggs

½ teaspoon dry mustard

Salt

2 cups whole milk or 1 cup milk and 1 cup cream

1 tablespoon unsalted butter

½ cup dry bread crumbs

Position a rack in the center of the oven and preheat to 350°. Lightly butter a 2-quart casserole. Bring 4 quarts of water to a rolling boil in a 6-quart pot. Toss in a small handful of salt and stir in the macaroni. Cook until it's slightly less than al dente, about 4–5 minutes or roughly half the time given in the package directions. Drain.

Put the hot macaroni in the casserole dish, add the cheese and ham, generously grind pepper over it, and gently toss until evenly mixed. Whisk together the eggs, mustard, and a large pinch of salt in a mixing bowl and gradually whisk in the milk. Pour it evenly over the macaroni.

Melt the butter in a skillet over medium-low heat and turn off the heat. Add the bread crumbs and toss until they've evenly absorbed the butter. Sprinkle them over the top of the casserole and bake until the crumbs are golden brown and the center is firm, about 30–35 minutes.

Baked Pasta with Ham, Mushrooms, and Rosemary

Fragrantly conjuring the changing leaves and crisp, clear air of autumn, this hearty baked pasta is perfect for supper on a cool fall evening but can also serve as a pasta course in a traditional Italian dinner. It's also a fine offering for a potluck dinner or buffet spread, since it can be made ahead and reheated. If you're offering it as a main dish, it need only be followed by a simple salad to make it a complete meal.

SERVES 6

2 tablespoons unsalted butter

2 tablespoons olive oil

1 cup ¼-inch-diced prosciutto, country ham, or cooked ham

2 large or 3 medium garlic cloves, lightly crushed, peeled, and minced

1½ pounds brown mushrooms such as crimini ("baby bella") or portabella, cleaned and sliced thick if small, diced if large

2 tablespoons chopped fresh rosemary

Salt and whole black pepper in a mill

1 pound short, tubular pasta such as ziti or penne, or small shells

½ cup freshly grated Parmigiano-Reggiano cheese, divided

2 cups coarsely grated whole-milk mozzarella cheese, divided

Bring 4 quarts of water to a boil in a 6- to 8-quart pot. Lightly butter a 9 × 13-inch casserole. Meanwhile, put the butter and oil in a large skillet over medium-high heat. When the butter is melted and bubbling, add the ham and sauté, tossing, until it has lost its raw, red color (if using country ham or prosciutto) or is hot through.

Add the garlic and sauté until fragrant, about half a minute, then add the mushrooms and toss until they're coated and have evenly absorbed the fat. Sauté, tossing, until they're colored and begin releasing the fat again. Add the rosemary and toss until fragrant, about half a minute more. Turn off the heat and season with salt and pepper.

When the water is boiling, add a small handful of salt and stir in the pasta. Cook until almost al dente, beginning to check it a minute shy of the cooking time on the package directions. It should be slightly underdone. Drain and immediately toss with the sauce and half of both cheeses, then transfer to the casserole. It can be made ahead up to this point. Let cool and cover.

When ready to finish the pasta, position a rack in the center of the oven and preheat to 400°. Uncover the pasta and sprinkle the remaining cheese over the top. Bake until bubbly and lightly browned on top, about 20 minutes. Serve warm.

Penne with Asparagus and Ham

This classic pasta sauce was originally paired with fresh egg fettuccine, but it's good to know that it also works well with short, tubular pasta such as penne for those times when you have neither the noodles nor the time to make them. It makes a fine main dish for lunch or supper but isn't too heavy to serve as a pasta course in a traditional Italian dinner, so long as the course that follows it doesn't contain ham or cream.

SERVES 4–6

1 pound asparagus
Salt
3 tablespoons unsalted butter
¼ cup finely minced shallots or yellow onion
4 ounces prosciutto or country ham, sliced ⅛ inch thick
    and cut into julienne
½ cup thinly sliced scallions, both white and green parts
Whole white pepper in a mill
Whole nutmeg in a grater
1 cup heavy cream
1 pound penne
1 cup freshly grated Parmigiano-Reggiano cheese, divided

Wash the asparagus and trim the cut ends. Peel the tough parts of the stems (the lower third) with a vegetable peeler. Cut off the tips and set them aside, then cut the stems in 1-inch lengths. Bring 4 quarts of water to a rolling boil in a 6- to 8-quart pot. Meanwhile, put the butter and shallots in a large, heavy-bottomed skillet over medium heat. Sauté, tossing often, until the shallots are just beginning to color, about 3–4 minutes. Add the asparagus stems and prosciutto and toss until the asparagus is bright green and the ham has lost its raw, red color, about a minute. Add the tips and scallions and toss until they're bright green. Add the cream, bring it to a boil, and cook until slightly reduced and beginning to thicken, about 2 minutes. Season well with white pepper and freshly grated nutmeg and turn off the heat.

When the water is boiling, toss in a handful of salt and stir in the pasta. Cook, stirring occasionally, until the pasta is al dente, and quickly drain it. Immediately toss it with the sauce. Add ½ cup of the Parmigiano and toss again. Serve at once with the remaining Parmigiano passed separately.

Penne with Ham, Rosemary, and Tomatoes

This is a pretty hearty sauce, and I find it too substantial to serve as a pasta course in a traditional Italian meal, but serve it as a main dish followed by a simple mixed green salad.

SERVES 4–6

---

3 tablespoons unsalted butter or 1½ tablespoons butter
  and 1½ tablespoons olive oil
1 cup small-diced cooked ham
1 medium yellow onion, split lengthwise, peeled, and
  diced small
1 large or 2 medium garlic cloves, peeled and minced
¼ teaspoon crushed red pepper flakes, or to taste
1 tablespoon roughly chopped fresh rosemary
½ cup dry white vermouth or dry white wine
2 cups canned Italian plum tomatoes, seeded and chopped,
  with their juices
Salt
1 pound penne or other short, tubular pasta or short
  fusilli (rotini)
1 cup freshly grated Parmigiano-Reggiano cheese, divided

Heat the butter (or butter and oil) in a 3-quart sauté pan over medium heat until hot and bubbly. Add the ham and sauté until it's beginning to color on the edges. Add the onions and sauté until golden, about 3–5 minutes. Add the garlic, red pepper flakes, and rosemary and toss until fragrant, about half a minute.

Pour in the vermouth or wine and bring to a boil, stirring and scraping the bottom of the pan to release any browned cooking residue, and boil until its mostly evaporated, about 3 minutes. Stir in the tomatoes, bring to a boil, and reduce the heat to a steady simmer. Simmer, stirring every now and again, until the sauce is thick, about 20 minutes. Turn off the heat.

Meanwhile, bring 4 quarts of water to a rolling boil in a 6- to 8-quart pot. Toss in a small handful of salt, stir, and stir in the pasta. Cook until it is al dente. When the pasta is almost done, gently reheat the sauce over medium-low heat.

When the pasta is ready, drain it quickly, being careful not to overdrain it, and immediately toss it with the sauce. Sprinkle ½ cup of the cheese over it, toss well, and serve immediately, passing the remaining cheese separately.

Ham Lo Mein

In Chinese cooking, to shred is essentially the same as the French to julienne: the food is thinly sliced and then each slice is cut into thin strips. The object here is to have the ham and vegetables in fine strips that are roughly the same thickness as the noodles. To do it, first cut the ham and vegetables into 2-inch-long pieces, then slice them and cut each slice into thin strips.

Chinese noodles are available in Asian markets dried, fresh, and precooked. Dried noodles are specified here, but you can also use fresh or precooked noodles in this recipe. Dried and fresh noodles are cooked just like Italian pasta. Precooked noodles are simply dropped in the hot water until they soften and separate. Unlike Italian pasta, Chinese noodles are always rinsed well after they're cooked.

If you aren't able to find Chinese noodles, thin spaghetti can be substituted for them.

SERVES 3–4

4–6 Chinese black mushrooms (dried shiitakes)
2 tablespoon light soy sauce, divided
1 teaspoon Chinese rice wine (not sake) or dry sherry
10 ounces dried Chinese noodles or thin spaghetti
2 teaspoons sesame oil
3 tablespoons peanut or canola oil
1 large clove garlic, peeled and minced
1 tablespoon grated fresh ginger root
1 cup shredded cooked Chinese ham or country ham (see headnote)
½ cup shredded scallions
1 cup shredded carrots
1 cup trimmed and shredded snow peas
3 tablespoons oyster sauce

Cover the mushrooms with hot water and let them soak until softened, about 15 minutes. Lift them from their soaking liquid, squeezing them dry over the bowl, and shred them into thin strips. Reserve the soaking liquid and mix 1 tablespoon of the soy sauce and the rice wine into it.

Bring 3 quarts of water to a rolling boil and drop in the noodles or spaghetti. Cook until al dente, about 3–6 minutes, depending on the noodles. Drain and rinse under cold running water. Drain well, put them in a bowl, and toss with the remaining soy sauce and the sesame oil.

Warm the oil in a wok, stir-fry pan, or deep skillet over medium-high heat and swirl it to coat the bottom and sides. Add the garlic and ginger and stir-fry until fragrant, about 10 seconds. Add the ham, scallions, carrots, snow peas, and mushrooms and stir-fry about 2 minutes.

Add the noodles and continue stir-frying until the noodles are hot through. Add the mushroom liquid mixture and oyster sauce and continue stir-frying until the noodles are evenly coated and fairly dry. Transfer to a serving bowl or individual bowls and serve at once.

Dressed for Dinner

HAM STEAKS AND COMPANY DISHES

On the fabled formal dinner tables of the Old South, and even on the humbler ones of simple farming families, a ham came to the company dinner table dressed for the occasion pretty much in only one way: boiled or baked whole and garnished with toasted bread crumbs or with a glaze and fanciful ornament of preserved fruit (see pages 13–18 for the methods). It was carved at the table. In some families it even remained in the dining room as a fixture on the sideboard until it began to look skimpy and shabby, and was then replaced with a new one. Back then, "fancy dishes" and "entrées" that contained ham were never served as a main dish. They were either used to round out the corners of a formal table that was laid in the old French style (in courses of multiple dishes presented all at once), or as a savory course before or after the main meat when the meal was presented Russian style—one dish at a time.

As entertaining relaxed and became less elaborate over the course of the twentieth century, however, those fancy dishes became the main event. What is more, others that would previously have been found only on the supper, breakfast, or family dinner table—for example, thick, broiled, baked, or pan-fried ham steaks—also began to turn up at company dinners.

Ham Steak Baked in Coca-Cola

The old recipes for ham in Coca-Cola (and yes, that's brand-specific) were developed before the formula was changed to include high-fructose sweetener. You can use a regular Coke for this recipe, but it's far better with one that's still made only with cane sugar, such as Mexican Coke.

SERVES 4

---

1 heaped tablespoon brown sugar
½ teaspoon dry mustard
Pinch of ground cayenne, or to taste
1 center-cut bone-in ham steak cut ½–1 inch thick
1 (12-ounce) bottle Mexican Coca-Cola

Position a rack in the center of the oven and preheat to 350°. Mix together the brown sugar, mustard, and cayenne in a small bowl. Remove the ham steak from the packaging and thoroughly drain away any liquid. Pat it dry.

Lightly butter a 9 × 13-inch baking dish and put in the ham. Rub the brown sugar mixture over the top and pour the Coca-Cola around its edges. Bake, basting occasionally with the pan juices, for an hour.

Transfer the ham to a platter and let it rest for 10 minutes before slicing. Using a wooden spoon or spatula, stir up the pan juices, scraping the dish to loosen any cooking residue, and pour them into a skillet. Put the skillet over medium-high heat and bring the pan juices to a rolling boil. Boil until they're reduced by three-fourths and syrupy. Turn off the heat and pour the pan juices into a sauceboat or small serving bowl. Slice the ham steak, drizzle it with some of the juices, and serve with the remainder passed separately.

Baked Ham Steak with Pineapple and Sweet Potatoes

When canned pineapple was first introduced, cooks probably went a bit overboard: up until then, pineapple had been a rare and expensive luxury. And there it was, not only affordable, but trimmed, peeled, cored, and neatly cut into rings. It soon began turning up in all kinds of "fancy" concoctions, but the most common was a sweet glazed hams studded with pineapple rings filled with maraschino cherries.

This recipe is of the same vintage, and may seem a little bit retro, but it's also a lot good. You could use fresh pineapple if you really can't stand the notion of the can, but trust me: by the time it bakes for an hour, you won't be able to tell the difference.

SERVES 4

---

4 medium, slender orange-fleshed sweet potatoes
   (about 1 pound)
1 center-cut bone-in ham steak (about 1¼–2 pounds),
   cut ½–1 inch thick, or 2 (8-ounce) boneless ½-inch-thick
   ham steaks
3 tablespoons unsalted butter, divided
1 (8-ounce) can pineapple rings, juice reserved
⅓ cup tightly packed dark brown sugar
1 teaspoon ground cinnamon, or to taste
Whole nutmeg in a grater

Scrub the sweet potatoes under cold running water, peel, and cut them into 1-inch-thick slices. If you can only find fat sweet potatoes, halve the potatoes lengthwise before slicing them. Position a rack in the center of the oven and preheat to 350°. Remove the ham steak from the packaging and thoroughly drain away any liquid. Pat it dry. Put 1 tablespoon of the butter in a deep, heavy-bottomed, oven-safe lidded 12-inch skillet or shallow flame-safe casserole. Warm the pan over medium heat and when the butter is melted and bubbling, add the ham and brown it well on both sides, about 4 minutes per side. Turn off the heat.

Arrange the sweet potatoes around the ham. Break the pineapple rings into quarters and scatter them over the potatoes. Stir the pineapple juice and brown sugar together and pour it over all. Dot the potatoes and pineapple with the remaining butter and sprinkle them generously cinnamon and nutmeg, both to taste. Cover tightly with the lid (or with foil if you don't have a lid for the pan) and bake until the potatoes are tender, about 30 minutes. Uncover, baste everything with the pan juices, and bake, basting occasionally, about 30 minutes longer, or until the pan juices are reduced and the potatoes are lightly colored.

Transfer the ham to a platter and slice it thickly or divide it into individual portions. Surround it with the potatoes and pineapple, spoon the pan juices over it, and serve.

Pan-Broiled Ham Steak
with Orange Sauce

Pan-broiling is a simple yet nice way to reheat fully cooked ham steaks, but even uncooked ham steaks take well to it. It's a dry heat method that differs from pan-frying and sautéing in that it involves very little if any added fat, only enough to keep the meat from sticking to the pan. The orange glaze is exquisitely simple and delicious, but you can omit it and make redeye gravy (see page 18) or just serve the ham with mustard passed separately.

SERVES 4

---

1 center-cut bone-in ham steak, cut ½–1 inch thick,
   or 4 (½-inch-thick) boneless ham steaks
About ½ tablespoon unsalted butter, bacon drippings,
   ham drippings, or vegetable oil
1 cup orange juice

Remove the ham steak from the packaging and thoroughly drain away any liquid. Pat it dry. Warm a heavy-bottomed 11- to 12-inch skillet, preferably seasoned cast-iron, over medium heat for 3–4 minutes. Add enough fat to barely coat the bottom of the pan.

Add the ham and let the bottom side sear until it's well browned and releasing from the pan, about 4 minutes. Turn and sear the second side, about 4 minutes longer. Reduce the heat and cook, turning once or twice more, until the fat is golden and crisp at its edges and the ham is hot through, about 3–4 minutes more. Transfer it to a warm platter and set it in a warm spot.

Add the orange juice to the pan, raise the heat to medium high, and bring it to a boil, stirring and scraping the pan. Boil, stirring often, until the orange juice is reduced to a syrupy glaze, about 3 minutes. Turn off the heat. If you like, you may enrich the glaze with a pat of butter. Slice the ham steak crosswise, spoon the orange reduction over it, and serve at once.

Chicken Rolls with Leeks and Prosciutto

The chicken's breast is its largest and leanest muscle, which has made it one of the most popular cuts on the bird. It can also be one of the dullest and driest cuts when it's handled indifferently or overcooked. Here, a bit of lean ham and a creamy filling of sautéed leeks bring out the flavor and keep this lean cut juicy and tender. Instant blending flour comes in a shaker. If you opt for using all-purpose flour instead, get a shaker with medium holes for dusting flour. It's so much more convenient and neat.

SERVES 6

---

6 small or 3 large young fresh leeks

6 boneless, skinless chicken breasts, trimmed of
    cartilage and fat

6 tablespoons unsalted butter, divided

2 tablespoons olive oil, divided

1 tablespoon chopped fresh thyme

2 tablespoons chopped flat-leaf (Italian) parsley

Whole black pepper in a mill

6 thin slices prosciutto

Instant-blending or all-purpose flour in a shaker

1 cup dry white vermouth or dry white wine

Lay the leeks on a cutting board so that the fanning upper leaves lie flat. Trim the root ends of the leeks and, one at a time, laying one hand on top of the leek to hold it steady, hold the knife parallel to the board and split them in half. Hold each half root-end-up under cold running water, fold back the layers, and wash away any dirt and sand. Drain and cut into 2-inch lengths, then cut each section into julienne.

Remove the "tenderloins" from the chicken breasts and set them aside for another use. Lay the breasts flat on a cutting board and, using a very sharp knife, cut them in half horizontally (parallel to the cutting board). Spread plastic wrap over a sturdy flat work surface, lay the chicken cutlets on it, and cover them with a second sheet of wrap. Lightly beat them out until they are a uniform thickness. Season with pepper and cover the cut side with a slice of prosciutto.

Put 1 tablespoon each of the butter and oil in a large sauté or braising pan over medium heat and add the leeks. Sauté, tossing often, until wilted. Add the thyme and 1 tablespoon of the parsley, toss until fragrant, and turn off the heat. Let cool slightly and then spread a spoonful of them over each cutlet. Beginning at the narrow end of each, roll them up and secure them with toothpicks or twine.

In the pan in which leeks cooked heat 1 tablespoon of the butter and the remaining oil over medium heat. When melted and bubbly, lightly dust the chicken rolls with flour, shake off the excess, and add them to the pan. Raise the heat to medium high and brown them well, about 2 minutes per side. Pour in the vermouth or wine and bring it to a boil, then reduce the heat to low, cover, and simmer until the chicken is cooked through, about 10–12 minutes.

Turn off the heat and remove the chicken rolls to a warm plate. Let them cool for 4–5 minutes, remove the toothpick or twine, and slice them crosswise into rounds. Arrange them on a platter or individual serving plates. Return the pan to medium-high heat and boil the pan juices, stirring and scraping the pan, until they're reduced to ½ cup. Turn off the heat, whisk in the remaining butter in bits and pour the sauce evenly over the chicken rounds. Serve at once.

Petti di Pollo al Forno all' Ilda
(Baked Chicken Breasts Stuffed
with Ham and Cheese)

In 1978 I was privileged to spend four months in Genoa, Italy, allegedly studying architecture, but in short order, I fell in love with Italian cooking. With architecture all but forgotten, I spent more time in the kitchen with Ilda, the Genovese woman who was our cook, than I did in the studio—a fact that ought to have told me something, but that's another story.

One of the first things she taught me was this simple baked stuffed chicken breast. It begins like a classic cordon bleu—boned chicken supremes stuffed with good ham and cheese and then rolled in breading. But then it takes a couple of important turns. Instead of sautéing or frying them, Ilda put them into a buttered casserole, poured in a little dry white wine, and baked them. It has been a staple in my own kitchen for more than thirty years.

SERVES 4

---

2 large boneless, skinless chicken breast halves, weighing
    about 8 ounces each

Salt and whole black pepper in a mill

4 thin slices prosciutto or country ham

4 thin slices Gruyère or Comté cheese, cut into approximately
    1- by 3-inch pieces

1 large egg

1 cup dry bread crumbs

About ¾ cup dry white vermouth or dry white wine

2 tablespoons unsalted butter

Position a rack in the upper third of the oven and preheat to 350°. Lightly butter an 8 × 10-inch casserole. Remove the "tenderloins" from the chicken breasts and set them aside for another use. Lay the breasts flat on a cutting board and, using a very sharp knife, cut them in half horizontally (parallel to the cutting board). Spread plastic wrap over a sturdy flat work surface, lay the chicken cutlets on it, and cover them with a second sheet of wrap. Lightly beat them out until they are a uniform thickness.

Turn the top (skin side) cutlets skin-side down (it won't matter with the other halves). Season lightly with pepper and lay a slice of prosciutto over each, completely covering it. Put a slice of cheese in the center of each and fold the cutlet around it, gently pressing together.

Beat the egg in a wide shallow bowl such as a soup plate. Spread the bread crumbs in a separate wide shallow bowl and lightly season them with salt and several twists of the peppermill. Roll each cutlet in the egg and lift it out, allowing the excess to flow back into the bowl, then roll it in the seasoned crumbs, patting gently so that the crumbs adhere. Lay them in the prepared casserole as they are breaded.

Carefully pour enough vermouth or wine around the cutlets to come halfway up their sides. Dot them with butter and bake in the upper third of the oven until they are golden, just cooked through, and the cheese is melted, about half an hour.

Prosciutto-Wrapped Salmon
with Fresh Tartar Sauce

Ham adds a savory depth to the meaty, assertive flavor of wild-caught salmon, but this is also nice with grouper, char, sea bass, or cod filets.

SERVES 4

FOR THE TARTAR SAUCE

1 cup mayonnaise, preferably homemade

2–3 teaspoons fresh lemon juice

2 tablespoons nonpareil capers, drained

1 tablespoon minced dill pickle

¼ cup finely minced scallions, both white and green parts

1 heaped tablespoon chopped fresh dill

Ground cayenne pepper or hot sauce

FOR THE FISH

4 (6- to 8-ounce) center-cut salmon filets (grouper, char, or cod would also work)

Salt and whole black pepper in a mill

Leaves from 2 healthy sprigs rosemary

8 paper-thin slices prosciutto, Serrano, or dry-aged country ham

Olive oil or melted butter

2 lemons, cut into wedges

To make the tartar sauce, blend together the mayonnaise and lemon juice until smooth, then fold in the capers, pickles, scallions, and dill. Season to taste with a dash or two of cayenne or hot sauce. Cover and refrigerate for at least 1 hour before serving (it will keep for up to a week).

Pat the fish dry and season lightly with salt and pepper. Sprinkle it with rosemary and wrap each with 2 pieces of the ham and secure it in at least two places with twine. Prepare a grill with hardwood coals or position a rack in the upper third of the oven and preheat it to 450°–500°.

If you're roasting, skip to the next step. If grilling, when the coals are ready, spread them out and place the grate 8 inches above the heat. Brush one side of the wrapped fish with oil and lay them on the grate, oiled-side down. Cover and grill 3–4 minutes, or until well seared on the bottom. Brush with more oil, turn the filets over, cover, and grill until the second side is seared, about 2 minutes. Move them to indirect heat and cook until done to your taste, about 5–10 minutes more per inch of thickness. Skip to the last step.

To oven-roast, rub a flat roasting rack with oil and fit it in a rimmed baking pan. Brush one side of the fish with oil, put them oiled-side down on the rack, and brush the tops with oil. Roast in the upper third of the oven until they're done to your taste—about 10 minutes per inch of thickness for medium to medium well.

Remove the fish from the grill or roasting pan to a platter, cut and remove the trussing strings, and let it rest 5 minutes before serving with the tartar sauce and lemons.

Rosa di Parma
(Ham-Stuffed Rolled Beef Tenderloin)

The tenderloin or filet is the long, round strap muscle that runs down either side of the spine of all vertebrate animals. It's the tender little round part of a chop or T-bone steak and the muscle from which filet steaks are cut. Because it gets very little action while the animal is alive, it's always tender; unhappily, that also means it's not as flavorful. Here, Parma's famed prosciutto takes care of that deficiency. There are probably as many versions of this dish as there are cooks in the city. This one is from Rosa Musi, a lovely Parmigiani grandmother who helped me master homemade egg pasta and a host of the region's stuffed pasta shapes. Although she did the braising the traditional way on the stove, it can also be done in the center of a preheated 350° oven.

Never store garlic infused in oil at room temperature or for more than a couple of days.

SERVES 6–8

4–5 large garlic cloves, lightly crushed and peeled
½ cup olive oil
3 pounds center-cut beef tenderloin
About 4–6 ounces thinly sliced prosciutto di Parma
About 4 ounces Parmigiano-Reggiano in one piece
Salt and whole black pepper in a mill
3 large fresh rosemary sprigs
3 large or 6 small fresh sage leaves
1 cup dry red wine
½ cup brandy or cognac

Wash the garlic, pat it dry, and put it in a heatproof bowl. Heat the oil in a small saucepan until very hot but not quite smoking and pour it over the garlic. Let it cool, then cover and steep for at least 2 hours or refrigerate for up to 2 days.

Trim the tenderloin and remove the silver skin (the fibrous connective tissue found at the thick end). Butterfly the tenderloin as follows: one-third of the way up its side, with the knife parallel to the cutting board, cut the tenderloin horizontally almost to the opposite side, leaving the same thickness attached on the side as from the cutting board to your cut. Open it to lie flat and beginning at the center of the fatter section, cut it horizontally as before so that the tenderloin unfolds like a letter and forms one large rectangle. Lay it open and lightly beat it to an even thickness with a mallet or scaloppine pounder.

Lightly brush the meat with garlic-infused oil and completely cover the surface with a single layer of prosciutto. Shave the Parmigiano cheese over the prosciutto with a vegetable peeler, completely covering it. Cover the cheese with a second layer of prosciutto. Roll the meat tightly and tie securely with twine in 4–5 places. Rub well with salt and pepper. Tuck the herbs into the twine ties. Put the tenderloin in a narrow pan that will hold it snugly and pour the remaining oil over it.

Brown the meat on all sides over medium-high heat, about 2–3 minutes per side. Add the wine and brandy or cognac, reduce the heat to medium low, loosely cover, and gently braise to desired doneness, about 30 minutes for medium rare, 45 minutes for medium. (This also can be done on the middle rack in the oven at 350°. Let the meat rest for 15 minutes before carving, then remove the string and slice crosswise into rounds: the slices will resemble the petal pattern of a rose, hence the name.

Prosciutto-Wrapped Pork Tenderloins

Pork tenderloin is the same cut as a beef filet and, just like its bovine counterpart, is lean and always tender, but is likewise the least flavorful part of the animal. It's also prone to be dry when mishandled. These shortcomings are handsomely corrected by simply wrapping it in prosciutto, which coaxes out and enhances its natural flavor and helps keep it from becoming dry should it happen to stay in the pot a bit longer than it should've.

SERVES 6–8

1 pair pork tenderloins (2–2½ pounds total)
Olive oil
2 tablespoons chopped fresh rosemary
3 large garlic cloves, finely minced
Whole black pepper in a mill
10–12 very thin slices prosciutto, preferably prosciutto
    di Parma
1 cup dry white vermouth
3 tablespoons unsalted butter
2 lemons, cut into wedges
Rosemary sprigs, for garnish (optional)

Trim the tenderloins and remove the silver skin (the fibrous connective tissue found at the thick end). Rub the entire surface of each lightly with oil. Sprinkle them with the rosemary and garlic, season generously with pepper, and pat the seasonings into the surface. Wrap each tenderloin with prosciutto, completely covering the surface. Truss each well with twine in five or six places. Set aside.

Position a rack in the center of the oven and preheat to 425°. Rub a small roasting pan with oil and put in the tenderloins. Drizzle them with more oil and roast for 20 minutes. Reduce the heat to 350° and roast until the meat registers an internal temperature of around 130–135° for medium (it will continue cooking as it rests), about 15–20 minutes longer.

Remove the tenderloins to a platter, loosely cover with foil, and let rest for 15 minutes. Deglaze the roasting pan over medium heat with the vermouth and let it boil until the liquid is reduced by half and lightly thickened. Add the accumulated juices from platter, turn off the heat, and swirl in the butter. Pour this into a warm bowl or sauceboat. Remove the twine from the tenderloins and thinly slice them. Arrange the slices on a platter, garnish with lemon wedges and sprigs of rosemary, if using, and serve with the sauce passed separately.

Saltimbocca alla Romana (Veal Scaloppine with Prosciutto and Sage)

"Saltimbocca" literally means "jump in the mouth" and is presumed to refer to its irresistibility, but the name might as easily be a nod to the way the lovely flavors dance on one's tongue. Though in Rome saltimbocca is traditionally made with veal scaloppine, it's also lovely with chicken breast cutlets (see Note).

SERVES 4

---

8 uniform veal scaloppine (about 1 pound), cut ¼ inch thick

Salt and whole black pepper in a mill

8–16 sage leaves

8 very thin slices prosciutto di Parma or other Italian-style ham

3 tablespoons unsalted butter

2 tablespoon olive oil

About ¼ cup instant-blending or all-purpose flour in a shaker

½ cup dry white vermouth or dry white wine

Spread a sheet of plastic wrap over a large cutting board and lay the veal flat on top of it. Cover it with a second sheet of wrap and lightly pound it with a meat mallet or scaloppine pounder until it is uniformly about ⅛ inch thick. Uncover and season lightly with salt and pepper. Lay 1–2 sage leaves over each piece of veal and then cover with a single slice of prosciutto, gently pressing it into the surface.

Put the butter and oil in a large, heavy-bottomed skillet (preferably nonstick) and turn on the heat to medium high. When the butter is melted and hot and its foaming has subsided, lightly but completely dust each side of the scaloppine with the flour, shake off any excess, and slip them into the pan, prosciutto-side down. Cook until golden brown on the bottom, about 2 minutes. Carefully turn them over with a spatula and cook about a minute longer. Transfer them to a platter.

Deglaze the pan with the vermouth or wine, stirring and scraping the bottom to loosen any browned cooking residue, and let it reduce slightly. Return the veal to the pan and simmer until the sauce is lightly thickened, about 2 minutes. Transfer the veal to a platter, pour the sauce evenly over it, and serve immediately.

NOTE ❋ This can be made with 4 (6-ounce) boned and skinned chicken breasts. Split them in half horizontally as directed for Petti di Pollo al Forno all' Ilda (page 110) and then prepare the cutlets in exactly the same way as the scaloppine.

Lunch, Brunch, and Supper

Back to that definition of eternity as two people and a ham: the dishes that follow sum up why that whole notion seems silliest to southern cooks. Like most cooks whose cuisine has been close to the land, for us, using up every scrap of leftovers so that nothing gets wasted isn't merely frugal, it's a point of pride and an outright art form. And nothing seems to inspire our creative juices quite like a bit of leftover ham. We toast both slivers and slabs of it in a pan lubricated with a little of the ham's fat. We mix it with leftover rice and fold it into pilau and jambalaya. We stir it into casseroles of potato, macaroni, and cubed leftover bread. We simmer it in rich sauces for ladling over toast points, biscuits, rice, and noodles. We chunk and grind it into salads and sandwich spreads, and layer slivers of it with toast and poached or fried eggs.

Most of these dishes are simple family fare. But thanks to the savory element of ham, even the humblest of them is lovely enough to be presented to company, especially when the meal is that odd twentieth-century in-between thing that we have come to call brunch.

Shrimp and Ham Jambalaya

Whether you call it pilau, pilaf, perlow, paella, or jambalaya, in the end, it all amounts to the same thing: rice simmered in an aromatic liquid that contains enough fat to keep its grains distinct and separate. The type of rice and technique may vary slightly—a paella, for example, is made with a short-grained rice and cooked in a wide, open pan, whereas most other variations use long-grain rice—but the basic idea is the same. In the South, the two primary versions are Creole jambalaya from Louisiana and pilau from the Carolina/Georgia Lowcountry. While cooks in both regions would argue that the two are not at all the same, the only substantive differences are their names and details of seasoning. The technique and proportions are identical.

SERVES 6–8

4 tablespoons unsalted butter or vegetable oil

1 large yellow onion (not a sweet onion), trimmed, split lengthwise, peeled, and diced

1 medium green bell pepper, stemmed, cored, seeded, and diced

2 celery stalks, strung and diced

12 ounces (2 cups) diced smoked ham

2 large garlic cloves, peeled and minced

1 tablespoon fresh or 1 teaspoon dried thyme leaves

¼ teaspoon hot pepper flakes, or to taste

2 cups long-grain rice

Salt and whole black pepper in a mill

4 cups ham broth (page 30), preferred, or chicken broth

4 tablespoons tomato paste

2 bay leaves

2 pounds large shrimp, peeled and, if desired, deveined

½ cup thinly sliced scallions, both white and green parts

3 tablespoons chopped flat-leaf (Italian) parsley

Put the butter or oil in a heavy-bottomed Dutch oven, preferably enameled iron, over medium heat. Add the onions, bell peppers, and celery and sauté, tossing often, until they're softened and beginning to color, about 5 minutes. Add the ham and toss until it's hot through and barely beginning to color, about 2 minutes more. Add the garlic, thyme, and hot pepper flakes and sauté until fragrant, about 1 minute.

Add the rice and stir until each grain is coated and hot. Season with salt and a generous grinding of pepper and stir in the broth, tomato paste, and bay leaves. Bring it to a boil, reduce the heat to a slow simmer, and cook until the liquid is nearly absorbed, about 8–10 minutes.

Scatter the shrimp over the rice, cover tightly, and turn down the heat as low as can be managed. Steam until the rice is tender and the shrimp are curled and pink, about 8–10 minutes longer. Add the green onions and gently fold them and the shrimp into the rice. Remove and discard the bay leaves, sprinkle with the parsley, and serve immediately.

Helen's Ham Fried Rice

In Chinese households, fried rice is a pick-me-up snack or late-night meal, never an accompaniment for another dish as it often is in Chinese American restaurants. This version comes from cooking authority Helen Chen, daughter of the legendary Joyce Chen. Its rich color is due to thick soy sauce, but if it's unavailable, Helen says you may use dark soy sauce but advises that the same amount won't color the rice, so add more gradually, taking care not to make it too wet or salty. My own substitution is a tablespoon of hoisin and dab of oyster sauce, but I'm a southern boy, so what do I know?

SERVES 3–5

1 cup fresh green peas or thawed frozen peas
1 cup diced carrots
4 cups cold cooked rice
2 large eggs
Salt and whole black pepper in a mill
4 tablespoons canola, corn, or peanut oil
½ cup thinly sliced scallion or diced onion
1 teaspoon thick soy sauce or Chinese dark soy sauce
½ cup diced cooked ham
1 cup fresh bean sprouts

Bring 6 cups of water to a rolling boil. If you're using fresh peas, add them to the pan and let it come back to a boil. Cook until the peas are almost tender, 4–15 minutes, depending on their freshness and age. (Precooking the frozen peas isn't necessary.) Lift them out with a skimmer and drain well. Add the carrots. Let it come back to a boil and cook them about 2 minutes, or until they're beginning to soften and drain well.

Put the rice in a large bowl and break up any lumps with your fingers. Beat the eggs in a separate bowl and season them to taste with the salt and pepper.

Pour the oil into a wok or stir-fry pan and place the pan over medium-high heat. When the oil is hot, but not smoking, add the scallions; they should sizzle. Stir for about 15 seconds. Stir the beaten eggs into the pan with a spatula and scramble until the eggs are dry and separate.

Add the rice to the eggs and mix thoroughly. Pour the soy sauce evenly over everything. Add the peas, carrots, ham, and bean sprouts and stir constantly until all the ingredients are well mixed and heated through. Serve immediately.

Ham, Asparagus, and Mushroom Strata

In the unlikely event that you've never encountered one, a strata is nothing more than a savory bread pudding: stale bread layered with cheese, savory vegetables, and traditional breakfast meats like bacon, ham, or sausage, and bound with an egg custard. Though most often served at breakfast or brunch, particularly at the holidays, they also make a lovely supper dish for a chilly evening in the spring or fall or, for that matter, at any time of the year.

SERVES 6–8

9 slices firm, home-style white bread
½ pound fat-stemmed asparagus
2 tablespoons unsalted butter
1 medium red bell pepper, stem, core, and membranes
   removed, diced
8 ounces brown (crimini or baby bella) mushrooms,
   cleaned and sliced
1 cup sliced green onions, both white and green parts
1½ cups diced cooked ham
2 tablespoons chopped fresh or 2 teaspoons crumbled
   dried oregano, divided
Salt and whole black pepper in a mill
Whole nutmeg in a grater
2 cups shredded sharp cheddar, Gruyère, or Swiss cheese,
   divided
1 cup freshly grated Parmigiano-Reggiano cheese, divided
8 large eggs
3 cups whole milk

Cut the bread into large dice. Butter a 9 × 13-inch casserole and put in half the bread. Trim the cut ends of the asparagus and peel the tough lower part of the stems. Cut the asparagus into 1-inch lengths, separating the tips from the stems.

Melt the butter in a heavy-bottomed skillet over medium heat. Add the bell peppers and sauté 2 minutes. Add the asparagus stems and sauté until they and the bell peppers are crisptender, about 3 minutes. Add the mushrooms, raise the heat to medium high, and sauté until they're opaque, about 3 minutes. Add the asparagus tips, onions, and ham and toss until hot, about a minute. Turn off the heat.

Scatter the ham and vegetables over the bread in the casserole dish. Sprinkle with half of the oregano and season well with salt, pepper, and nutmeg. Sprinkle half of both cheeses evenly over the ham and vegetables and top with the remaining bread.

Whisk together the eggs, milk, and remaining oregano and season well with salt, pepper, and nutmeg. Pour the custard over the entire casserole, cover with plastic wrap, and let it sit until the bread has fully absorbed it, about 15–30 minutes, or refrigerate it overnight. Let it sit at room temperature for 30 minutes before baking.

Position a rack in the center of the oven and preheat to 375°. Uncover the strata and bake until it's almost set, about 25 minutes. Sprinkle with the remaining cheese and bake until golden, about 10 minutes longer. Let rest 10 minutes before serving.

Grits Casserole with
Ham and Cheddar

Southern cooks have devised many ways of using up leftover grits, but this traditional casserole isn't one of them. Here, the grits should be freshly made and still quite hot. The good news is that this casserole reheats beautifully and can therefore be made up to two days ahead. Let it completely cool before covering and refrigerating it. Let it sit at room temperature for about half an hour before reheating it in the middle of a preheated 350° oven.

SERVES 6

---

1 cup raw hominy grits or whole corn grits (see Note)
2 cups coarsely grated extra-sharp cheddar or
    Gruyère cheese, divided
2 tablespoons unsalted butter
2 cups chopped cooked ham
1 cup thinly sliced scallions, both white and green parts
Pinch of dry mustard
Salt and whole black pepper in a mill
4 large eggs, lightly beaten
½ cup light cream
½ cup whole milk

Bring a teakettle filled with water to a simmer. In a heavy-bottomed 2- to 3-quart saucepan bring 4 cups water to a rolling boil over medium heat and slowly whisk in the grits. Cook, stirring, until the water returns to a simmer. Reduce the heat to a steady simmer and cook, stirring occasionally, until the grits are thickened and tender, 30 minutes for quick grits or 1 hour or more for regular or whole corn grits. If the grits get too dry before they're tender, add a little of the hot water from the kettle to them as needed. They should be quite thick.

When the grits are almost ready, position a rack in the center of the oven and preheat to 350°. Rub the inside of a 3-quart casserole with butter.

Off the heat, stir 1½ cups of the cheese and the butter into the hot grits until the cheese is melted and evenly mixed with the grits. Fold in the ham, scallions, and dry mustard, taste, and season well with salt and pepper.

In a separate bowl, whisk together the eggs, cream, and milk, then gradually stir this into the grits mixture. Pour the mixture into the prepared casserole and sprinkle the remaining cheese over the top. Bake until the casserole is set in the center, about 30–40 minutes.

NOTE ❋ This quintessentially southern hot cereal is made from ground dried corn kernels. There are two basic kinds: hominy grits and whole corn grits. Hominy grits are coarsely ground hominy (corn kernels from which the tough outer hull has been removed); whole corn grits are, as you would expect, the whole kernel, hull, germ, chaff and all, again coarsely ground. Stone-ground means the grits have been milled with an old-fashioned millstone. Though both types are cooked the same way, their cooking times will vary. There are three kinds of hominy grits: regular, quick, and instant. Quick grits have been par-cooked and dried so that they cook faster, but not as fast as their package directions claim. Instant grits have been fully cooked so that they only have to be reconstituted before they're fed to the pigs, which is all they're fit for.

Ham (or Ham and Turkey) Tetrazzini

Historians and popular culture mavens like to argue about the origins of this popular casserole, but all agree that the dish was created for Italian soprano Luisa Tetrazzini, whose appetite was apparently as large as her legendary voice. The original wasn't a casserole but a bed of spaghetti topped with a velouté sauce enriched with poultry, mushrooms, and possibly slivered almonds, and finished with grated Parmigiano-Reggiano cheese. For at least three-quarters of a century, however, the more usual rendition has been this crumb-topped casserole. Here in the South, the poultry is often either supplemented with ham or altogether replaced by it. If you're buying ham rather than using up leftovers, choose cooked ham that isn't "smoky" or sweet.

SERVES 6

3 cups chicken broth

1 cup water

1 herb bundle made with 1 bay leaf tied with 2 sprigs each of
    flat-leaf (Italian) parsley and thyme

6 tablespoons unsalted butter

8 ounces small fresh white or brown mushrooms,
    brushed clean and sliced

5 tablespoons all-purpose flour

1 cup whole milk or light cream

Salt and whole white pepper in a mill

Whole nutmeg in a grater

8 ounces spaghetti

2 large egg yolks, lightly beaten

¼ cup dry sherry

3 cups diced cooked ham or 1 cup cooked ham
    and 2 cups cooked turkey

½ cup slivered almonds, lightly toasted

½ cup freshly grated Parmigiano-Reggiano cheese

1 cup dry bread crumbs

Bring the chicken broth, water, and herb bundle to a simmer in a heavy-bottomed saucepan over medium heat. Simmer until the liquid is reduced to 2 cups and turn off the heat. Remove and discard the herb bundle. Meanwhile, position a rack in the center of the oven and preheat to 375°. Rub a 9 × 13-inch casserole with butter and bring 4 quarts of water to a boil over medium-high heat.

Melt 5 tablespoons of the butter in a large, deep skillet or sauté pan over medium-high heat. Add the mushrooms and sauté until they begin to color. Sprinkle the flour over the mushrooms and cook 1 minute, stirring constantly. Gradually whisk in the broth and milk or cream and bring to a simmer, stirring constantly. Season to taste with salt, pepper, and nutmeg. Simmer until it's thickened and the flour loses its raw, pasty taste, about 3–4 minutes. Turn off the heat.

When the water is boiling, stir in a handful of salt and the spaghetti. Cook until almost al dente. Drain and put it in the prepared casserole. Fold the egg yolks, sherry, ham, almonds, and cheese into the sauce and pour it over the pasta. Gently toss to mix and level the top with a spatula.

Melt the remaining butter in a skillet over low heat. Turn off the heat and add the bread crumbs. Toss until the butter is evenly absorbed; sprinkle the buttered crumbs over the top of the casserole. Bake until lightly browned, about 30 minutes, and serve hot.

Potato Gratin with Ham and Sage

This is a perfect gratin for entertaining because it can be done ahead and is practically effortless. While most traditional potato gratins are made with cooked potatoes, this one forgoes the preliminary cooking (and extra work and dirty pot that it generates). The potatoes are simply peeled, sliced, and tossed together with caramelized onions, ham, sage, grated cheese, and cream. The baking time is longer, but after all, that's unattended time, which means you're free to deal with the rest of dinner or, better yet, relax with your company.

SERVES 10

2 tablespoons unsalted butter

2 large yellow onions, trimmed, split lengthwise, peeled, and thinly sliced

2 pounds (about 4 large) russet (baking) potatoes

2 cups heavy cream

2 ounces (about one $\frac{1}{8}$-inch-thick slice) country ham or imported prosciutto, cut into fine julienne

2 tablespoons chopped fresh sage

$2\frac{1}{2}$ cups grated Gruyère cheese

Salt and whole white or black pepper in a mill

Whole nutmeg in a grater

Position a rack in the center of the oven and preheat to 400°. Generously butter a 10 × 15-inch, 2½- to 3-quart gratin or baking dish (I use an enameled iron 3-quart gratin dish).

Melt the butter over medium heat in a large skillet. Add the onions and sauté, stirring occasionally, until tender and evenly colored a deep gold, about 10–15 minutes.

Meanwhile, peel and thinly slice the potatoes with a sharp knife, mandoline, or food processor. In a large bowl, mix the potatoes with the onions, cream, ham, sage, and 2 cups of the cheese. Season with salt, pepper, and nutmeg to taste and toss well.

Pour everything into the prepared casserole, pressing it down and leveling the top, and sprinkle with the remaining cheese. Bake for 15 minutes and reduce the heat to 350°. Bake for about 60–75 minutes longer, or until the potatoes are very tender and bubbly at the center and the top is golden brown. Serve hot or warm.

Ilda's Ham and Potato Gratin

On my first day in Italy, our class spent the day sketching in the picturesque port towns of Portofino and San Frutuoso. Soaked with Riviera sunshine and salty Ligurian air, we were very hungry, as only active young people can be. Our cook, Ilda, had long since gone home, but she left something for supper that she called casseruola al forno, *which just means "baked casserole." We popped it into the oven and made a salad. As its aroma filled the house, there was something very familiar about it. When at last we sat down to supper, I took a bite and was enveloped by the memory of a dozen covered-dish suppers back home. Our exotic Italian casserole was only scalloped potatoes with ham, a dish I'd cut my teeth on.*

SERVES 4–6

---

2 pounds boiling potatoes, peeled and sliced about
  ¼ inch thick
4 tablespoons unsalted butter
4 tablespoons unbleached all-purpose flour
3 cups milk, heated
Salt and whole white pepper in a mill
Whole nutmeg in a grater
1 cup small-diced boiled ham, preferably one that is not
  smoky or sweet
1 cup grated Gruyère cheese (see Note)
¼ cup freshly grated Parmigiano-Reggiano cheese

Put the potatoes and enough water to just cover them in a heavy-bottomed pot over medium-high heat. Bring to a boil, reduce the heat to medium, and cook until the potatoes are barely tender, about 8–10 minutes. Drain and set them aside until they are cool enough to handle. Position a rack in the upper third of the oven and preheat to 375°.

Melt the butter in a saucepan over medium heat. Sprinkle in the flour and whisk until smoothly blended. Slowly whisk in the hot milk and whisk until it begins to thicken. Reduce the heat to low and simmer, stirring frequently, until thick and the flour has lost its raw, pasty taste, about 5–10 minutes. Season to taste with salt, pepper, and nutmeg and turn off the heat.

Lightly butter a 9-inch-square casserole dish and cover the bottom with a layer of potato slices. Scatter about a third of the ham over them. Spread a third of the sauce over this and top it with a third of the Gruyère. Add another layer of potatoes, ham, sauce, and Gruyère and repeat with a third layer, finishing with the remaining sauce and Gruyère. Sprinkle the Parmigiano over the top and bake in the upper third of the oven until the top is golden brown and the casserole is bubbly at the center, about half an hour. Serve hot.

NOTE ❋ In the South, most traditional cooks use cheddar cheese. If you prefer it, substitute 1¼ cups of sharp cheddar for the two cheeses called for above.

Acknowledgments

In a funny way, this little collection of recipes spans nearly four decades of cooking and writing about food. To try to thank everyone who has been involved in a lifetime of learning and growing as a writer and cook would be foolhardy, even if there was enough space to do so. But I must single out the long line of editors who have nurtured me as a writer: Erica Marcus, Harriet Bell, Janice Easton, Sydny Miner, Beth Cheuk, Katie Benoit Cardoso, Amy Lyons, and now, Elaine Maisner at UNC Press, who I especially thank for her belief in my work in southern food and its history and for including me in this series. Thanks also are due to the UNC Press team who were involved in putting this book together, particularly my vigilant copyeditor Mary Carley Caviness. Thanks also to Josh Rayburn and Andria Segedy, my editors at the *Savannah Morning News* during this project, and to the loyal readers of my regular columns in that paper, all of whom patiently endured so many stories about ham over the last year. I also must thank friends and colleagues Helen Chen and Michele Scicolone, the former for invaluable advice and guidance on Chinese cooking, and the latter for her wisdom on all things Italian. I also thank my parents, who have never stopped believing in me and have never complained about all those years of architecture school that ended up giving way to a completely different career.

Finally, a special thank you to Timothy Lindsay Hall, who has filled my heart and home life with so much joy and peace, and has never once complained about all the ham he had to eat over the last year. He met each test run cheerfully, unflinchingly pointing out things that weren't up to par, and enthusiastically praising each dish that succeeded.

Index

DISCARD